RELATIONSHIP BANK ACCOUNT

How to Make Friends, Have Fun, and Attract Lifelong Success

BY

JEFF FENSTER

FREE GIVEAWAY

Get your copy of Jeff's Network to Millions Playbook

Just scan above to instantly get access!!

"I've personally witnessed Jeff start many companies in wildly different industries, and quickly rise to the top of that industry because of his relationship capital. This book is a roadmap so you can do the same. If you are an aspiring entrepreneur or leader, this is a must read!"

DAVID MELTZER
Co-Founder Sports 1 Marketing
Former CEO Leigh Steinberg Sports Agency

"Jeff works with investors, franchisees, athletes, entertainers and 1000's of employees!! That is why is he is so qualified to write the book and teach Relationship Capital!"

DAN FLEYSHMAN
Founder Elevator Studio

"Relationship Capital is the one investment that always returns 100X more all others. Jeff Fenster is a master at building relationship capital and has proven it by building multiple 8 figure companies. This book shares his proven strategies and an easy-to-follow model so you can too. I highly recommend Jeff and this book!!"

ROLAND FRASIER
DigitalMarketer.com, Scalable.co, EpicNetwork.com

"Ready to jumpstart your career and grow your business without being salesy or sucking up? Read this book! Most leaders get to the top and keep the secret sauce to themselves. Jeff Fenster does it right in Relationship Capital. In it, Jeff breaks down his success so that any student, entrepreneur, business leader or parent can quickly and authentically grow their influence."

GABRIELLE BOSCHÉ
Bestselling Author
co-CEO, The Purpose Company

DREAMSTARTERS

www.DreamStartersPublishing.com

Table of Contents

About Jeff Fenster

Jeff Fenster is an award winning entrepreneur who credits his success to one thing: the art of building and maintaining relationships. After graduating with his J.D. from Thomas Jefferson School of Law,

Jeff focused his energy on innovation and business development. His business creations range from a quick serve restaurant chain (Everbowl), construction company (WeBuild Stuff) Payroll & HR company (CanopyHR),and a digital marketing Agency among others. He was named a top 100 Entrepreneur in America under the age of 35, a Top 40 Executive under 40 by the Business Journal, a finalist for CEO of the year by Ernst & Young and was named a Top Entrepreneur to follow for 2022.

He has appeared on over 500 podcasts, created courses on entrepreneurship and relationship capital for for LinkedIn Learning, and speaks on stages across the country on entrepreneurship. Jeff's acclaimed podcast, The Jeff Fenster Show features successful entrepreneurs, celebrities, and athletes sharing their insights and stories of success.

Foreword by David Meltzer

I often speak about how to differentiate objective and subjective value, but there is one area of our lives where this task becomes difficult.... our relationships. Relationships come from everywhere, especially in the digital age, where a click, tap, or swipe is seemingly all it takes to make an initial connection. Because beneficial relationships can come at us at any time, we've got to be consistent and persistent in how we connect with others.

Know that every place you go, all it takes is one conversation to change the rest of your life. That is why I mention to everyone the importance of being prepared with a question (or two) to stimulate interest when meeting people for the first time. Smile, make eye contact, and ask something that will naturally create some curiosity or emotional connection between you and the other person. A good rule of thumb is to focus on putting out the energy that you want in return, so consider asking questions that you would like to be asked, or questions where you are genuinely interested to hear an answer. Listen to what they've got to say and then follow up with additional questions, because listening aligns you with this new connection and the values that they hold dear.

There will always be a difference between simply connecting with people and developing a lasting relationship full of objective and subjective value, and some of my most valuable connections apart from my family have come from mentor/mentee relationships.

When I was a child, one of my most important mentors was my grandfather, who taught me the three things you need in life to be happy. My grandfather's best advice, "You need to find one partner who is your liaison between you, your family, and your friends. You need to find one job that you love. And, finally, you need to buy the best bed that you can find." These words have served as been one of the guiding forces of my life. I was also able to learn quite a bit from legendary super-agent Leigh Steinberg (the inspiration for *Jerry Maguire*), during my time as CEO of the Leigh Steinberg Sports & Entertainment agency. I not only learned Leigh's three best tips for negotiation, "Never negotiate to the last penny, always be fair, and don't do business with dicks,") but that relationship also brought life lessons which I carry with me every day, including the drive to be kind to my future self with every action I take.

While managing and developing our relationships can seem like a tall task, this all comes down to practice. Practice by consistently and persistently surrounding yourself with the circumstances you desire. Practice asking questions to stimulate interest and then make emotional connections with others. This will empower you to build lasting and beneficial relationships with mentors and mentees who value the same things that you value, people who operate with the same principles, who will push you to be the best version of yourself.

What I've come to realize in recent years is that I've not only gained valuable insights as a mentee, but as coaching and mentoring have become an even greater part of my life, I have grown as well. One of my longest-lasting and most beneficial relationships as a friend and mentor has been with this book's author, Jeff Fenster, who I've known since he was young. Working with him over the decades has helped me become a better listener, as well as a teacher. As Jeff grew from a young man into the successful entrepreneur, father, and husband he is today, each of us have grown to better understand the true power of Relationship Capital and how to grow it, develop it, utilize it, and leverage it.

This book is a blueprint for you to follow so that you can start building and developing Relationship Capital in your life. It will provide you all of the value and knowledge that Jeff has learned and used in his career – so you can do the same.

David Meltzer

What does relationship capital mean to you and how has it helped you in your life?

The value of being kind to your future self by doing good deeds. Allowed me to manifest what I wanted rapidly and accurately.

Would you rather have $1,000,000 in cash or know 1,000 people very well?

1,000 people very well.

Describe your relationship with Jeff Fenster.

Family! He is my little brother. I've known him for 35 years and have watched him grow from a little kid to an entrepreneurial rockstar.

Introduction

Listen, I know what you're thinking. Hundreds of books have been written on this topic in one form or another. What makes this book so unique?

First, this book is based on personal experience, not hyperbole. In addition to my own experience, I can point to hundreds of success stories, from those who have gone through my courses to those who consulted with me privately. The ideas I present here aren't "theories" of business; they work, and they work well, on one condition.

If you work the work, and walk the talk, you WILL succeed. I'm a "no-excuses" kind of guy, and I (frankly) roll my eyes when I meet people who have "tried this and that" with no success. Nine times out of ten, they're not being honest. Not with me, and, most importantly, not with themselves.

Sadly, this is the norm. Yes, it's true; only a few businesses reach the very echelon of success. Think of the Amazons, Teslas, and Apples of previous generations. However, the reality is that EVERY company has the potential to make a dent and bring its creators, investors, and customers a better life. A much better life – both financially and emotionally.

As we unroll the ideas for creating Relationship Capital to change your business, life, and legacy, I want you to be incredibly honest with yourself. I'll take you through all the steps, but you have to take them. Some of them are simple - easy, almost. Others will challenge you and force you out of your comfort zone because that's where success lies. That's where your true calling will reveal itself.

We'll start with defining what Relationship Capital is in the first place. Then, how can you use it to leverage success in your business and life? We'll also be covering:

• How Relationship Capital can help you excel
• Your Relationship Capital "bank account" and how it looks, and how it can be used to build your fortunes (literal, figurative, and otherwise)
• The purposes of Relationship Capital and how it can buy you access that you NEED
• How Relationship Capital can buy you OPPORTUNITIES
• How it can buy you TIME
• And, maybe most importantly, how Relationship Capital can buy you CREDIBILITY

We can talk about what Relationship Capital can do for you for thousands of pages, but that's almost like talking about what a billion dollars can do for you. So, in the second part of this book, we'll get into:

12

- How to develop Relationship Capital (from the very beginning to ultimate fluency)
- Why you need to "dig the well" before you're thirsty
- Why being interested is more important than being interesting
- How to make deposits in your Relationship Capital bank account
- Leveraging the power of your Relationship Capital account

Remember that people buy from friends. In some ways, this is the crux of the power of Relationship Capital. We've all heard it a million times: people buy from people they know, like, and trust. You create those relationship with others using the ideas discussed in this book and that I discuss in my coursework.

Bonus chapters will include:

- The bug light concept
- How to be the expert in anything

Who am I to be telling you what to do? What makes me "special?" First, I don't think I'm special. I'm just an ordinary guy who figured out what extra stuff I had to do to become extraordinary. At heart, I'm a humble man who, with a bit of luck and a lot of sweat, created a world for myself that I couldn't have dreamed of when I was a kid. After sweating through law school and graduating, it became clear that law wasn't meant for me. Instead, I had an entrepreneur's heart, mind, and spirit.

I guess you could call me a serial entrepreneur. I've been recognized nationally for various businesses I've created, ranging from Everbowl – a national quick-serve food chain, WeBuild Stuff – a construction and fabrication company, CanopyHR – a payroll and HR firm to JFEN Holdings – a relationship-based digital marketing agency, amongst others.

I was named a top "100 Entrepreneurs in America Under the Age of 35" in 2013 by Empact and a "Top 40 Executive Under 40" in 2019 by The Business Journal. I was also a finalist for "Entrepreneur of the Year" in 2020 by Ernst and Young and in 2019 for "CEO of the Year." I am also an instructor on entrepreneurship and have created multiple courses for LinkedIn Learning. In addition, I'm a mentor for San Diego State University's Lavin School of Entrepreneurship, a guest on 100's of business podcasts, and speak on stages around the country.

All these activities have allowed me to combine my passions for entrepreneurship and helping people. Just like my coursework, my goal is to help others. To help you. The bottom line is to help you understand how to develop, use, and leverage relationship capital and do the 'extra' like me, so you can be extraordinary. I can't do the work for you, but I can guide you and demonstrate how I and hundreds of my students and clients have used the concept of Relationship Capital to create their personal fortunes and freedoms. I'm not just referring to money. I know that money doesn't buy happiness, but we also know that it does make life easier. What "buys" happiness is your Relationship Capital. We are happier when we have meaningful relationships with those around us. Relationship Capital is a way to transform that happiness into true personal happiness, coupled with endless opportunity, choices, and ultimately, financial independence.

Before we begin, I want you to take stock of where you are today. Are you happy? Are you healthy? Are you financially secure? Are you where you want to be or where you thought you'd be at this point in your life? What's been missing? What are you doing to improve your life? What AREN'T you doing?

That last sentence is the most important. Before you can have anything good in your life, you must take responsibility for what isn't working. This is different from blame, as that helps no one. There are always things we can do differently, and if we ignore them, we are doomed to make the same mistakes over and over.

As you turn the page in this book, commit to turning the page in your life. Anything you haven't done that you knew you needed to do, ends now.

- You will do what it takes.
- You will walk the talk.
- You will be true to your relationships.
- And you will succeed – in life and in business.

Along the way, you'll create a personal legacy that will inspire others around you – even people you've never met and will never meet.

Are you ready?

Chapter 1

What is Relationship Capital?

Here's the truth – you can succeed at anything in life.... even if you don't have any experience, money, formal education, or know-how. You can get everything you need with 'Relationship Capital.' This is the tool used by all the superstars that no one realizes.

Many people don't even know what Relationship Capital means, but that's the purpose of this book. I want everyone who reads this book to leave with an understanding of what Relationship Capital is, why it's so important to your life, how to grow and develop it, and ultimately, how to leverage it.

Why do you see so many good ideas fail? Why do hard-working, experienced entrepreneurs fail? The truth is, it's not **WHAT** you know or know **HOW** to do the job…. it's **WHO you know.**

I can hand most entrepreneurs a million dollars and watch them blow it. But, if I provide them with the right introductions or connections, I don't need to give them a penny, and I can watch them exceed and excel. So, as we explore what Relationship Capital is and how it can work in your life, I think you'll see and recognize how other big names in the business world have used it to succeed.

Does everyone use Relationship Capital to make millions, change lives, and succeed? Of course not, but that doesn't mean they shouldn't. For example, suppose you can make a million dollars a year in your business without tapping into what we'll discuss. In that case, you could probably make two million or even ten million with it. It truly is that powerful!

Relationship Capital is the most critical skill to success across all aspects of life, not just for entrepreneurs. Unfortunately, while there is a succinct definition of this concept, it misrepresents what Relationship Capital is all about. It's not enough to say "this" is Relationship Capital – it's a process of building an army of people who are genuinely fans of YOU and your mission.

We see people constantly advancing up the ladder of success or getting opportunities that we don't think they deserve or should be ours. We might see someone get a promotion because they're "so-and-so's" best friends or the niece or nephew of the boss. We tend to complain about it and even blame others for our lot in life, but what you're really feeling and saying is, "They're only succeeding because they have the Relationship Capital that I don't." You failed to recognize that even if you're more qualified, paid more dues, want more, or even need more, Relationship Capital trumps all these things. It's the secret door or fast lane to bigger and better opportunities. It turns walls into doors and, when used correctly, can allow you to succeed at anything you want in life.

The moment that you accept it and embrace it is the moment when your life will change.

To reiterate the point, even more, you see this in popular culture, even when relationships are strictly virtual. If a Kardashian poses or talks about a product you sell, you will instantly get a ton of eyeballs looking at it and possibly buying it. That is why brands pay them so much money to endorse their products. Think Michael Jordan, Nike, or Gatorade. With this being said, you have two options – you can either pay these influencers a ton of money (which you will need to have or raise) to endorse your products, OR you develop influential friendships that can get you the introduction to a popular influencer or athlete.

This applies even if you aren't an entrepreneur or working for a company. Politics in the corporate world aren't about the trade of power or money; instead, they're about the trade of relationships. Who knows who and how good those relationships are.

When I started my career, I quickly realized that people with many friends and big contact lists were successful. But, of course, that wasn't a coincidence. If you had many friends and contacts, you weren't making cold calls; you were calling people you knew. So when the rapport is already there, you don't have to build it; you have to nurture it.

People buy from people. They make decisions based on their comfort level with you, not just with the product or service you are pitching. As you develop more relationships and increase your Relationship Capital, success starts to "fall in your lap." It becomes a system that compounds over time. Thus, the more Relationship Capital you develop, the more you continue to receive.

After graduating from law school and deciding I wasn't going to pursue a legal career, I had a serious issue. I had six figures in law school loans to pay back, a fiancée, and a two-year-old daughter to support. So naturally, I did what any person would do in that situation and got a job. It wasn't my dream job, but I needed the money, so I got a job selling payroll services for ADP. I was given a $38,000 salary plus commission. I owed $1100 a month in student loans, so I knew I had to figure out how to quickly make a lot of money!

I set a goal to be the number one sales rep in the company. I didn't know anything about selling payroll services, but I knew some basics of selling, so I first looked up who the number one sales rep in the company was. It was a guy in the Midwest who had made and developed a relationship with a franchiser of a major restaurant chain. He had built the relationship at the very top level of that company, so every single current and the new franchisee (and they had thousands of them) had to sign up for payroll services through this guy. He had a built-in flood of incoming deals and didn't have to sell anything to any of them, only to that one decision-maker at the top. Since he had built a relationship with that one person, he could sell millions of dollars in payroll services.

I came to realize there were gatekeepers to deals. While my contemporaries were selling to small-business owners, I started focusing on relationships and building rapport with accountants, CPAs, insurance agents, and bankers. Why would I do that? Well, every business owner has a CPA. Every business owner has a banker that they work with. Every business owner needs insurance. So, if I made friends with and added value to the new business account banker, he would recommend me to every business that opened an account with him. If I had a great relationship with a highly regarded CPA in the community, she would recommend me and my payroll services to every business she worked with. This strategy was all contingent on IF I built Relationship Capital.

How did I do it? First, I identified the top bankers, CPA firms, and insurance agencies in San Diego and scheduled meetings with them. I let them know that I met with new and existing business owners every day. Then, I laid out a plan to recommend that particular bank, CPA, and insurance agent to my prospects and clients. I'd tell them, "I'm going to bring all my customers to you. I meet with business owners and decision-makers all day, and many haven't opened a bank account or hired a CPA yet. They need a bank account and a CPA to sign up for our payroll services. So, I'm willing to send all of my new businesses to you, and in exchange, when you encounter a business that needs payroll services, you refer them to me."

The pitch was simple: We were going to be a team. We knew how to care for each other's clients and ensure a better cohesive experience for them. Furthermore, they would take our recommendations highly because each business trusted one of us on the team (either me on the payroll side, the banker, or the CPA).

Only some people want the same bank, CPA, or even payroll company, so I would build out my team by enlisting a top business banker at multiple banks and with multiple CPAs. I would ask my customers if they preferred a bank or

CPA/Accounting firm before I would mention any names or provide my contacts. For example, if they mentioned, "I only do business with ABC Bank," I would say, "Perfect, I work with Mary at this branch, and she'll take great care of you. This will all work seamlessly."

When I started my payroll company, a CPA firm referred almost 80 clients to me during my first two years in business. Why? Relationship Capital. One lunch with him, showing him how we worked and did things, plus bringing him ten clients that day, sealed the deal. I led with value. Not "What can you do for me?" but rather, "What can I do for you? How can we work together?" (More on that later.)

My two core values and business principles are making friends and having fun. So I build Relationship Capital by making friends with everybody, regardless of my or their status in life. I don't sell you, and I don't ask you to sell for me. We're friends; of course, we'll help each other out.

You have to look at relationships differently – yes, they need to be sincere, honest, and meaningful. But it would help if you also looked at them as investments with ATM machines attached. They can result in introductions, connections, advice, exposure, and money – no matter who you know or what you do. People naturally want to help each other and give. You'll find success when you focus on what you can give and receive and how to develop relationships where you can give and receive.

Now, this might sound selfish, but all relationships technically are. Even in my relationships with my children, I want them to be happy. That's a selfish feeling because I'm happy when they are and want to be happy. Relationship Capital is about giving. By giving more value than we receive and making friends, you will build Relationship Capital.

Drew Brees

What does relationship capital mean to you and how has it helped you in your life?

Relationship capital is by far the greatest resource you can possess. I'm sure if you asked any successful entrepreneur, business person, or athlete, they would immediately acknowledge the team behind it all. Regardless of where you are in your life, you have arrived at this point based on the knowledge, experience, wisdom, and mentorship of so many others.

I am certain where I am as a quarterback in the NFL, with so many coaches and teachers along the way who have helped to instruct me, both on the field and in life. From a business perspective, it is through strong relationships and partnerships that great companies are built. The motivation, inspiration, and perspective that is brought to a company through those relationships and partnerships is what keeps it innovative and constantly pushing forward. Everyone has different strengths and expertise, and being able to lean on these unique skills at various points along the way is what pushes the team through each level.

Would you rather have $1,000,000 in cash or know 1,000 people very well?

Without question, I would rather know 1000 people very well. These types of relationships are what bring incredible value to our lives. Both as someone who can receive guidance and mentorship, but more importantly, how you can help guide and mentor others. It is the cycle that keeps pushing our society forward. Taking the lessons and experiences we have been taught to further our knowledge, understanding, exploration, and discovery. And then passing that on to others. It continues to raise the bar.

Describe your relationship with Jeff Fenster.

I have always admired Jeff's entrepreneurial spirit and his desire to build teams and companies. I believe he is one who appreciates the journey, values the relationships he is building and is always striving to push the envelope. His best is yet to come.

Build Your Relationship Capital

What is your Relationship Capital like right now?

_____

_____

_____

_____

_____

How do you want it to improve? How can you make it improve?

_____

_____

_____

_____

_____

"Be genuinely interested in everyone you meet, and everyone you meet will be genuinely interested in you."

Rasheed Ogunlaru

Chapter 2

How to Excel with Relationship Capital

The beauty of Relationship Capital is that it's a currency. It's very much related to money, whether cash, crypto, or otherwise. The more of it you have, the more you can accelerate and excel in your career. We've already mentioned this, and I'm sure you've heard it before, but who you know is more important than what you know, and who you know is also more important than what you have.

If you know the right people and are an employee in a corporation, you can accelerate your career and earnings with Relationship Capital. If you are self-employed and an entrepreneur, you can accelerate the growth of your company and your finances with Relationship Capital. In addition, you can navigate any politics in any organization, whether it's your own company, a corporation, or even a volunteer role, with Relationship Capital. You will gain the exposure you would never have achieved and can find your way to the top with Relationship Capital.

By building up your Rolodex with Relationship Capital, you can excel quickly. Back to my ADP days, for a minute, I went to my friend David Meltzer, bestselling author, CEO, and co-founder of Sports 1 Marketing and host of the podcast "The Playbook." Here's someone I knew in a high place. We were friends, and I knew I needed his help to succeed in my new position; I needed to connect with business owners. Since I was young and just out of law school, I didn't know ANY business owners personally.

After David and I met for lunch, he emailed 500 of his contacts, introducing me and saying what a great favor they could do for him by meeting with me. No pressure. No sales. No gimmicks. No strings attached. Just an introduction. From that one email from David, I closed 92 accounts and generated almost $55,000 in commissions. I used those deals, plus the others I worked on, to become the #1 sales rep in my office and the country within the first two months on the job. This all happened from just that one lunch.

You might think I got lucky. But what most people don't realize is that I created that luck. I had spent the last twenty years building Relationship Capital with David for that moment, which allowed me to excel. That allowed me to 'get lucky,' and I've used this tool to keep getting lucky with each new endeavor I undertake.

The Beginnings

Here's an example of developing Relationship Capital. I met David Meltzer when I was just a kid and he was in high school. David's mom and my mom worked together and were best friends. I watched him play high school football and was a big fan of his. For some reason, he took a liking to this little kid, and in some ways, I think he recognized that we had similar personalities. Growing up, he always hung out with me when our families reunited.

When I became a teenager, my interest in business and sales brought us together again. Since I had a strong drive to learn, I asked him if I could intern at some of his companies. At that time, he had an interior door company, one of the first video applications for the internet, and another company where he flew CEOs and CFOs of organizations to retreats and workshops. I did anything he let me do, from bringing those CEOs food and water to picking up trash, mowing his lawn, and babysitting his kids. Before I understood what Relationship Capital was, I knew that David was someone I admired. I knew that by spending time with him and observing him, he could help teach me to become successful in business.

That teenager didn't know I would need David to help start my career; I just knew that this was someone I liked, cared about, and wanted to learn from. What I got out of the "deal" was a great friendship and mentorship. I understood I needed to know many people and build solid, real, authentic relationships with them. I was focused on **learning over earning**.

Networking

Many people try to build a network and develop Relationship Capital. They go to networking meetings or join networking groups in that effort. However, they often make the biggest mistake that you can make. They try to create inauthentic networks, and it never works. In fact, I think this does more damage than good because people pick up very quickly that you're not being authentic. So they will stay away from you with a twenty-foot pole and won't refer anyone to you.

I hate going to networking meetings for this reason. They're about as deep as picking up someone at a bar for a one-night stand; and, frankly, are a waste of time. Everyone at those networking meetings has an angle and something to sell – they don't want to network or build relationships. They want to sell to you, and it's not authentic.

Instead, I want to go to a coffee shop, sit with someone, and get to know them. Let's learn about each other. Let's talk. How can I help you? The goal is the other person, not how many people I can meet who might help me do something or get somewhere. There's a huge difference between "knowing" someone and having and building a relationship. It's not just about a handshake, an exchange of business cards, and then moving on to the next. It's about investing time, energy, thought, care, and even more time into nurturing a real relationship.

How Can I Help?

This is the paradigm shift between knowing someone and creating a relationship. When your thought process changes from 'how can you help me' to 'how can I help you,' you are in a position to excel via Relationship Capital. You can now build real relationships; the perfect relationship is when both parties work within that framework.

I once heard a saying about personal relationships that I think applies here:

"You know you're in a great relationship when each of you secretly thinks you got the better end of the deal."

Right? If you're in a relationship with someone, and you think you got the better end of the stick, and the OTHER person feels that same way, you're golden. The same applies here as well. If you're in a mutually sincere and legitimate relationship with someone who can help you excel in your career, and they think that they scored because they have a relationship with you, that's a perfect balance. You can only feel this way if it is sincere because it's not about "How is this person helping me?" It's about "I'm so glad I have this person in my life – I'm so lucky to know them."

You're helping them, and they're helping you; it's a win-win, and it's real. It's what friendships and relationships should always be about. Both parties feel fortunate to know each other and feel lucky when they have a chance to help the other person. You know you'd do anything for your best friend and/or partner. You do it because you care about them. You do it, not looking for a return of favor but because you know, they would do it for you, too. Those are your lifelong friends.

Establishing this type of relationship is similar to business. You're not best buddies, but you are in an authentic relationship where you truly WANT to help the other person. Not with the desire or motivation to "get something back," but because you want to nurture a relationship. In time, you will receive something, but that's not why you go into it. You go into it to learn, to help, and mutually guide each other. You want them to succeed, and they want you to succeed.

The more friends you have versus business relationships, the difference. Business relationships could be more paper thin. I want to have friends and make sure we're all successful – that's the difference between "networking" and Relationship Capital, and that's what I'm trying to get at in this book. It's all about how to make friends, have fun, and build your Relationship Capital, so your net worth is your network.

When you have a true-blue friend, you never question their motive. Friends do things for you, and when they do, you don't say to yourself, "Hmm, I wonder what this guy is gunning for." Instead, you accept and appreciate the friendship. On the other hand, if you have a business relationship for the sole purpose of networking, your "connection" might do something for you, and your innate defense mechanism might ask, "Ok, what's their motive? What are they trying to get out of this?" Your walls go up, making it difficult for business or money to flow.

Instead, when you're friends, it's almost automatic. There is no second-guessing. The key is trust, and with that trust, both parties, both friends, know and trust each other. Both have an open mind and heart when opportunities arise that can benefit one, the other, or both.

Let's say you and I met at a conference or networking meeting. I talk about myself and what I do and then say, "Hey, can you introduce me to one of your top clients?" What am I exposing as a person? First, I'm shallow. Second, I want something from you. Third, I'm not interested in you at all. I'm clearly only interested in what you can do for me.

How many times have you attended a networking event (meeting people who might do or refer business with you) and had that mentality? What can these people do for me? If you're being honest with yourself, you know you've been that person, "that guy or that girl." We've all done this.

The key is to ONLY do business with friends. The old adage to never do business with friends isn't true anymore. Especially in today's social media inundation of surface-level "friendships," it's easy to forget what a real friend looks like and feels like. It's easy to think you don't want to "mix" friendship and business, but I'm here to tell you to throw that old saying out the window.

I don't care who you are or what you do. I will only do business with friends because I don't want to worry about ulterior motives. I only want to do business from a shared space of abundance, trust, friendship, and fun. When you can create that type of space with a whole bunch of people, now you have Relationship Capital. It's a happy place in more ways than one. I have a tribe of people who have helped me with my success, helped me get back on my feet quickly when

I've fallen, and cheered me on through it all. They're my ignition and parachute; in turn, I'm theirs. I'm there to help them be successful. THAT'S Relationship Capital, and THAT's what I want to teach you.

Friends

Not too long ago, I hired a teenager, Ben, to be my first employee at Everbowl. When Ben started, he didn't have any business acumen and was raw around the edges, but I saw great energy and potential in him. I knew I could help him develop into a Rockstar and someone successful, like many had done for me when I was his age.

Ben wanted to break out and try something else a few years after working for me. He started selling Kangen Water machines. Of course, I wanted to support him, so I bought one. He was doing pretty well, but after we started offering Everbowl franchises, he came back to me to see if he could buy one. Again, my belief in him from his unwavering 'what can I do to help' and constant desire to learn attitude made me want to help him even more. I wanted to help him succeed in life and get everything he wanted!

Unfortunately, he couldn't afford to buy a franchise from us at that time. Fortunately, Ben had built Relationship Capital with me, Everbowl, and the entire Everbowl executive team. As a result, we decided to finance him and not let his lack of capital stand in his way.

Ben became Everbowl's first franchise partner! At the time of this writing, he's in his early twenties and crushing! However, he is looking at buying his second store from us, this time without needing our financing.

I'm sure he'll make me some money over the years, and I'll make him some money, but the entire "transaction" is based on friendship. An authentic friendship. A friendship that is rooted in the foundation of Relationship Capital.

I'm willing to help all my friends make it in whatever way I can because it's all about leading with value. It's all about giving without the expectation of receiving anything in return.

Dan Fleyshman

What does relationship capital mean to you and how has it helped you in your life?

Whenever someone asks me, "what's your superpower?" I ALWAYS answer the same way, by pointing at my phone. It's helped me at every stage of life, in every aspect, from a dinner reservation to raising money for charity.

Would you rather have $1,000,000 in cash or know 1,000 people very well?

If I know 1,000 people well, then $1 million would be peanuts.

Describe your relationship with Jeff Fenster.

I proudly bet my money, time, name, and relationships on him to win the championship. He is everything I look for in an entrepreneur to bet on.

Build Your Relationship Capital

Where in your life are there opportunities for your Relationship Capital to excel?

_____

_____

_____

_____

_____

How can you create more opportunities?

_____

_____

_____

_____

_____

"Two kinds of people have many friends, one with bank balance and the other with boldness."

Amit Kalantri

Chapter 3

Your Relationship Capital Bank Account

When you think of your bank account, you can picture it as a ledger. It's either a positive number, zero, or negative. Of course, we equate that to money. We don't want a zero balance, nor do we want a negative amount in that account. When we think about relationships, it's critical to think of them as a bank account. I would, in fact, argue that it's just as tangible as a money-based bank account.

If you constantly make withdrawals without ever adding money or making deposits, your account will be at zero or negative. This is the same with relationships. If you're withdrawing via too many favors, not following through, or asking someone to do something for you without ever giving back, you'll be in the negative balance with your Relationship Capital account.

We all know this type of person. We only hear from them when they need something. They're only nice to us when they have a favor to ask. They keep withdrawing from our relationship account until we finally start to get frustrated to the point that we cut things off. We may be "friendly" with them when we see them out and about, but we're putting our energies elsewhere. They are the type of person who takes and takes so much that you don't want to be around them anymore.

Then, other people always want to help. When you need something, they're there for you. Even when you don't ask for help, they ask how they can help, or they volunteer to help. They're not looking for anything from you when helping you out – it's just their nature to be this way. They've built a positive relationship bank account with you, so you'll do anything for them when needed.

Most relationships fall into the zero balance – no one tries to withdraw anything, but no one gives much of anything. In these types of relationships, there really is no relationship. It's paper thin; you're "broke." This obviously exists with strangers because you don't know them, and they don't know you, but it can also happen in business and personal relationships. Too often, I see businessmen or businesswomen try to "get a favor" from someone they don't know or barely know.

Think of your old high school "friend" who contacts you out of the blue to tell you about their new "business opportunity." They're trying to spend their perspective of Relationship Capital to gain your interest and money. They "know" you, think, and then believe that this gives them the capital to approach you. Unfortunately, they are mistaken. They are merely intruding and using a thin connection to make a withdrawal where there's zero balance, to begin with.

When someone in your life is a giver, who has worked on and invested in Relationship Capital with you, you feel like you owe them. They don't have that perspective, they don't think you owe them anything, but you do, and that's what Relationship Capital is all about. You'll go out of your way to introduce them to people they need to meet or resources that will help them.

Your job in business and life is to be that giver – to be the one that is helpful to other people. Not just to "give back," although that will happen, also, you'll build meaningful relationships. These relationships will make you feel good, supported, and valued. We all need to feel like we matter in our world and to those around us. So put, making deposits in your Relationship Capital account feels good.

At some point, when you're not looking or asking, someone will "pay you back." Maybe it's helping you with a personal issue or making an amazing business connection. Maybe it's someone offering you your dream job because they are in a position to hire and think of you. Maybe it's someone asking you to be on their literal stage as they give a talk about business success. Maybe it's someone inviting you to write a forward to their book. It can happen when someone sends you business by referring their clients to you. It can also happen when tragedy strikes your life, and people reach out to support and help you through difficult times.

Relationship Capital can literally be a lifesaver... and it can certainly be a career saver.

Connections

When I started in sales, I knew that even if I didn't have the specific language for this concept, Relationship Capital was the key to my success. I understood that I had to be honest and sincere in making connections. As I've said, I like making friends and having fun in both life and business. (Aren't they really the same thing?)

Let me share a little example – a snippet from my life that you might see in your life...

For years, I went to the same grocery store down the street from where I lived. I often saw the same woman at the checkout line, Linda, and I would always talk with her when I was in line. We would chit-chat about local things, kids, work, you name it. Just a nice, casual friendship and friendliness that never left the grocery store. I would take two or three extra minutes each visit to foster and nurture that connection.

Now, did we do any explicit "favors" for each other? Nope. But we had an authentic relationship because it wasn't just a "let me out of this small-talk circle." We had sincere and authentic chats and conversations. We made micro-investments into each other's lives with time and energy, so we had Relationship Capital built between us. I felt like I knew her, and she felt like she knew me.

Fast forward three-and-a-half years, and I have my own payroll company.

During one of our conversations, she said to me, *"Hey, you started your own payroll company, right? My brother's company is looking for a new payroll provider. Can I introduce you?"*

"Absolutely, sure!"

In my mind, this company was relatively small, and while it would be a nice account, not too much would come of it. But instead, it ended up being one of the biggest accounts I

44

had ever gotten in my career. It was handed to me on a platter because I spent time getting to know someone at the corner grocery store. Someone who had no obvious or apparent "value" to my profession and didn't care – I liked them, and that's all that mattered. I wasn't looking for value or "what I could get out of" that relationship. I just enjoyed it. I enjoyed the connection with another human being.

Having a positive balance with any human being is good. It's just a really good thing. The more positive balances you have with more people, the bigger your tribe is. The bigger your tribe is, the bigger your support system is. From there, opportunities fall on your head solely because you have people positively thinking about you.

Why People Resist

People out there don't put time into relationships unless they think they will benefit in some way. A great example of this is the first time I spoke on stage. I was in San Diego about to speak to about two hundred people. I was in my usual attire, a backward cap and casual clothing. Everyone else was in formal business attire. Before the event, I mingled and tried to talk to people, but most people looked over and past me. They wanted to talk to someone they thought would add more value to their life than they thought I could. They might have thought I was in the wrong room, for all I know.

Once I stepped on stage as one of the key speakers, you should have seen the looks on people's faces - the ones who overlooked me, who considered me to be "not valuable" to them. I didn't appear to be "anyone." Instead, they were now here to listen to me. They missed the opportunity to get to know me before I was on stage, and suddenly, they wanted to talk to me.

In fact, my talk was about relationships in business, and I opened the talk with how many people had ignored me, looked away, or rushed me off when I tried to talk to them. "You chose not to talk to me because you didn't think I was anyone of value." They had prejudged and predetermined how much value I could bring to their life, and they judged me wrong.

"That's why you don't build authentic relationships - your networking doesn't work. That's why you can't quickly and immediately build an authentic relationship with someone who might be able to help you someday."

We make this critical error by asking someone the usual two qualifying questions: what do you do, and where do you live. People use these two questions to qualify their audience and determine how much energy they want to invest in this conversation. If I say, "I'm a gardener," most people don't want to talk to me. If I say, "CEO of Microsoft," everyone wants to talk to me. I'll be honest, that gardener might start their own business and need your services, or that grocery clerk's brother might own a huge company who can use your services. Prejudging someone based on what they do or where they live is hugely limiting your Relationship Capital.

ALWAYS REMEMBER, EVERYONE IS SOMEONE'S BROTHER, SISTER, COUSIN, AUNT, UNCLE, MOTHER, FATHER, OR FRIEND! Just because the person in front of you isn't the homerun contact you want ◊ doesn't mean they don't have a connection that could change your life.

Once I stepped offstage, everyone wanted to talk to me. Before, people didn't see my value to them because of how I looked. They were wearing blinders that didn't allow them to see and understand that EVERY connection with another human being holds value. Everybody can help you in your life, just like you can touch and positively affect everyone. If you approach humankind with the desire and effort to make as many friends as possible, you open opportunities you couldn't have otherwise been exposed to. You build a tribe, and you become inviting of people instead of pushing them away because they don't fit what you think "value" looks like.

Otherwise, you think you can't "catch a break." When, really, you just haven't created that opportunity or that "break."

When you build authentic relationships, you invite financial gains, even without trying.

Neil Patel

What does relationship capital mean to you and how has it helped you in your life?

Relationship capital is the sum of all the value you've built from your relationships. And over time, as you keep helping people, you'll build up more credit (value)... over time, you can leverage that value to get help in exchange.

Would you rather have $1,000,000 in cash or know 1,000 people very well?

$1,000,000. With average S&P returns, you can live off the money for life.

Describe your relationship with Jeff Fenster.

I've known Jeff and his family for years. He's a good friend you can count on whenever you need help.

Build Your Relationship Capital

What does your Relationship Capital bank account look like?

_____

_____

_____

_____

_____

In what ways are you wearing blinders to people?

_____

_____

_____

_____

_____

"You win more friends by granting a favor than by asking for one."

Frank Sonnenberg

Chapter 4

The Purpose of Relationship Capital

Maybe you've heard of "Six Degrees of Separation" as a concept about how we're all connected to each other. This idea posits that you are connected to anyone else by six degrees of separation or connections. So, for instance, you and I might be connected by someone you know who knows someone that I know.

This mental exercise became popular via the actor Kevin Bacon, and it's a great "game" to play. Essentially, how many steps between one actor and Kevin Bacon is the "Bacon Number." There's even a board game and "rules" to the exercise. The claim is that any actor, even a more "obscure" artist, can be linked to Kevin Bacon with six mutual connections. Most well-known actors, dead or alive, can be linked within 2-4 connections. For instance, the late Henry Fonda has a Bacon Number of 2: Henry Fonda was in the movie *Midway* with Robert Wagner. Robert Wagner was in the movie *Wild Things* (1998) with Kevin Bacon. Two connections.

Beyond Kevin Bacon, this idea has some real truth for your life. It comes down to "I know a guy, who knows a guy, who knows a gal, who knows a guy." Play your cards right by creating real relationships; before you know it, you're standing in front of Kevin Bacon or whoever you need to meet. The concept of "six degrees of separation" may be a myth, but I know there's a truth to it that can help you personally and professionally.

Let's talk about this and the value of Relationship Capital…

As we've discussed, knowing many people means more doors are open to you. From those doors come more opportunities. These doors and opportunities get opened for you no matter your lot in life, your specialty, your expertise, or your niche. It doesn't matter if you sell real estate, are a lawyer, or are an engineer – I would predict that if you look at anyone successful in your field, they have a high level of

Relationship Capital. Mind you, there are exceptions. Some people get to the "top" without Relationship Capital, but they are the exception – not the rule.

Generally speaking, though, if you show me someone with a big social network of good, quality relationships, I'm going to show you someone who is extremely successful. That's the purpose of Relationship Capital – your job is to build genuine relationships. At the end of the day, in this capitalistic United States of America that we live in, people buy from people, people promote their friends, and nepotism is real.

You Are the Company

I'm sure something like this has happened to you. You get off a long flight for a business trip and go up to the rental car company's counter to get your car. The clerk behind the counter is just plain rude. Maybe she had a bad day, or maybe the customer before you was a jerk, and she's still trying to shake the experience off. But the bottom line is that you weren't treated well. You might rightfully walk away from that experience thinking, "I'm never going to rent from ABC company again – what assholes."

Now, the company didn't do you wrong, necessarily, that clerk treated you poorly. But you don't tell yourself and others, "Jill at ABC company was terrible." Instead, you turn

53

your experience with Jill into the entire company. Jill is the company. Unless the company reaches out to you proactively or responds very well to a complaint that you express, you're not likely to go to them again.

Likewise, if you have had a terrific experience with someone, even if the service is "so-so," you might rave about that company or organization. Think of a restaurant where the service was top-notch from beginning to end, but the food was just "ok." You're still likely to head back there because you had a great experience. You're not going to say, "Tim at that restaurant is amazing," you're going to say that the service there is great, and the restaurant is a fun place to go to.

People, as individuals, hold way more power to sway the image of their company or group than they might think. The same goes for their inner and outer circle. Whether you're generous and kind or polarizing, people's tribes are built on Relationship Capital. The more Relationship Capital you have, the more opportunity you have. They go hand in hand.

Network as Net Worth

We buy from each other. We buy from friends. We even see this with "friends" we've never met. The fact is that they're people we relate to in one way or another, and we will buy from them or buy whatever it is they're plugging. You buy Air Jordans because you want to be like Michael Jordan – you feel comfortable with his face and image. That's why companies pay big money to score major endorsements from highly regarded celebrities. They bring comfort to the consumer, so the consumer goes, "Michael Jordan drinks Gatorade, so I'll drink Gatorade." That's Relationship Capital.

You might not have a budget to pay Michael Jordan, but what if you're friends with someone who knows his trainer? Maybe you can build Relationship Capital to the point where there's a picture of Michael Jordan using your product. Those types of things occur because of relationships. It's who you know that can easily help you navigate this world. But unfortunately, it's an unused currency that most people do not use.

Sometimes someone will say something like, "Well, you're only there because you know so-and-so." Yeah? That's right. I do know "so-and-so." So why don't you know "so-and-so" why aren't you friends with them?

If you're connected to "high-value" individuals, you've been screened in a way. If you're friends with someone who other people aspire to know and admire, you must be "ok." You're adding value to that "high-value" individual, so people know you can add value to your life. Higher-value people have a lot of fake people hanging around them, but all they really want is authenticity, and they don't get it. For instance, the most beautiful or handsome individual often doesn't get asked on a date because people are intimidated by them. A celebrity like Dwayne "The Rock" Johnson is surrounded by people who want to be around him. They don't actually give a shit about him as a human being, so he wants authenticity that he won't get from those people. He's got his walls up, but if you're friends with him, he'll lower his walls for you to get to know him.

Treat Your Boss Like Your Friends... and Your Friends Like Your Boss

You're a little uneasy if you treat your boss like most of us do. You may not tell them what you really feel since you want to tell them what they want to hear. You may be afraid to show your vulnerability since they might see it as a weakness. However, if you are honest with them and show your boss that you can be trusted and that you understand your strengths and weaknesses, you'll find opportunities exponentially increase. You've created an authentic relationship with them, and you're a human being to them. You will build a connection where you and your boss are now friends. You've built Relationship Capital.

Likewise, if you treat your friends with the same respect that you would treat an admired boss, you'll find yourself with lifelong friends who would drive across the country if you needed help.

Both your friends and boss who know you know that you're better at what you do over time. They will recognize you for your expertise and wisdom when they recognize this. The same holds true with Relationship Capital – it might not seem comfortable or fluid when you first start practicing it. But, over time, you can perfect the craft of building honest, sincere, and mutually beneficial relationships to advance your life and business.

The key is knowing and understanding that everyone out there is connected. So, back to Kevin Bacon's six degrees of separation, we're all connected to someone else, who's connected to someone else. So, make good connections and nurture relationships across all facets of your life. The purpose of Relationship Capital, then, can be used as a tool strategically in your life. As you do this, your credibility and your value rise.

Be valuable to valuable people. You'll become a better person and get exposed to new ideas and perspectives, shaping your understanding of different cultures and groups. It will keep you out of your comfort zone and out of a bubble where you are only mixing with people who are like you and who think, look, and sound like you. Ultimately, you will become a better human being. You'll be exposed to more diverse and better conversations. You'll learn things you would never have learned before. You'll have more opportunities that you would never have seen before, possibly taking you in directions you wouldn't have imagined.

You will also learn who you don't want to spend too much time with. You will find yourself drawn to people who are givers versus takers. You can't be friends with everyone, and it's ok; you can still be kind. I don't hold grudges. If someone wants to mend fences with me, it's easily done. Holding grudges and having negative emotions are a waste of time. This is a world of abundance, and I want everyone to succeed.

Brad Lea

What does relationship capital mean to you and how has it helped you in your life?

It means the world to me. To put a definition on it, I would say "Relationship Capital" is the total value derived from utilizing relationships. Sometimes, it's not what you know but who you know. At the end of the day, the more hands you shake, the more money you make. It has been instrumental in my life financially, mentally, and spiritually. I wish more people understood the value of relationship capital.

Would you rather have $1,000,000 in cash or know 1,000 people very well?

Tricky question, Jeff. Depends on the people. If those 1,000 people were all high-caliber people, I would take relationships. That also assumes that "knowing them well" is meant positively; however, if those 1,000 people were degenerates with no integrity, I would take the million dollars.

Describe your relationship with Jeff Fenster.

I've known Jeff since 2020 and the relationship is highly valued. I consider Jeff one of those high-caliber types, and I am grateful to know him. Its been great watching how he has impacted the world and I am excited to continue to strengthen our friendship and do business together.

"My philosophy to life is very accommodating. I am ok with making friends with all manners and classes of people. I am more concerned about what is on the table."

Vincent Okeke

Chapter 5

Relationship Capital Can Buy You Access

I have a confession – even though I'm writing this book, you should probably know that I'm not very computer savvy. This is funny to many people since one of my more recent and most successful ventures was a digital marketing agency. My friends laugh at me, knowing that when I started, I barely knew how to turn a computer on, let alone be a digital marketer.

I bring this up because it's important to illustrate how Relationship Capital can put you in a position where you can succeed, even without experience. For example, how can someone like me, far from being an expert in digital marketing, succeed to the point where I won two 6-figure contracts within three weeks?

Relationship Capital.

Maybe you've heard of Neil Patel. Neil not only co-founded two great companies, KISSMetrics, and Crazy Egg, but he's also a *New York Times* bestselling author, named a top influencer by the *Wall Street Journal*, a Top 100 Entrepreneur Under 30 by President Barack Obama, and a Top 100 Entrepreneur by the United Nations. The guy is a rock star in the digital marketing arena. Google him if you don't know his name and reputation.

Proximity to Power

It was 2011, and I just knew the digital age was upon us, and more and more companies needed to improve their digital footprint. The future of business was going online, and I wanted to capitalize on it. I had just sold my payroll company and recruiting agency and was looking for my next venture. As I mentioned, I didn't know much about computers or who Neil Patel was, but I knew I wanted to own my own digital marketing agency.

I thought about who I did know that could help me get started, teach me some things, point me in the right direction, or even partner with me.

I realized I had an old childhood friend, Pat Flynn, whom I grew up with, who could help me. His work was in digital marketing, albeit in a different realm. He has a thriving online business called smartpassiveincome.com, where he showcased how he made money with smart passive online businesses that generated excellent income. So I reached out to him and asked if I could hire him to consult and teach me how to make money on a computer.

"My company is about passive income," Pat told me. *"I'm not the guy to help you. Instead, you should work with Neil Patel."*
As a marketing rookie, I had yet to learn who Neil Patel was.
"Who?" I said
Pat laughed and said, *"If you want to work in digital marketing, you should probably know who Neil is. He's a rock star. Would you like me to make an introduction?"*

I went home that night and looked Neil up. Wow! I knew that if I had Neil on my team, I could get anyone to sign up for the new venture. Shortly after, Pat made the intro and got me a one-on-one meeting with Neil.

Step one was complete, and I had a warm introduction to Neil. Now I'm sure that Neil gets a million people asking and taking from him, but the mistake they make is not offering value. I was not going to blow this introduction and fall into the crowd. Before I met him, I considered what value I could provide him. I was great at sales! I had a large rolodex of business owners who were friends and had used my payroll or recruiting services. I would go and sell a few accounts before I met Neil and demonstrate my ability to generate business (a.k.a., make him money and save him time). When we had our first call, I said to Neil, "Great to meet you. I have a 6-figure check from our first customer with your name. Where would you like me to send it?"

Neil laughed out loud and was so taken aback by the approach he wanted to meet me and better understand if I was as crazy as I sounded or if I was for real. The value angle I provided him at that moment separated me from the rest.

I always lead with value when I start new relationships. So let me tell you how THAT came about.

Opening Doors

Before I met with Neil and Pat, my first connection for this idea was with an old family friend named Barry.

Barry was a friend of my parents whom I'd known since I was a little kid. As I got older and interested in business, I was drawn to Barry and did everything I could to learn from him. He was very successful, and I would always pick his brain. Barry would advise and patiently sit down with me, even when I was just in middle and high school. Over all those years of talking and learning, we became friends and built significant Relationship Capital. Barry had Relationship Capital that I didn't, and I had some that he didn't.

Finally, after many years, I had a reason to make a "withdrawal" from my account with Barry. We hadn't ever done any direct business at this point, but I knew that Barry had access to CEOs of major firms. He knew decision-makers who could help me get my new digital marketing efforts. Through his introductions, I got my first 6-figure contract, and Barry helped me open doors I couldn't have otherwise. My relationship with Barry bought me access to major players. Those contracts let me leap from being a digital marketing unknown to partnering with the top marketer in the world – Neil Patel.

After my conversation with Pat, when I knew I had a real connection to Neil, I scored a second 6-figure contract. I told them that Neil and I would work nonstop to make sure they increased their revenue. I was so confident in our abilities that I offered to get started with no upfront costs to them but secured a six-figure contract that would only be paid if we showed results. They happily agreed to the arrangement.

With that contract "in hand," I went to my meeting with Neil and told him I had that contract in hand based on working together. I told him I would pay him out of my own funds before we received any money to have him work with me on the contract. I had the 'in' with Pat. Neil knew Pat and knew that if Pat was ok with me, he could be ok with me, too. So I led with value (which I keep encouraging you to do) – a literal "check" out of my own money, in good faith, knowing we would succeed.

And we have.

Chain Effect

This is all about chain effects. The chain effects will come naturally and organically if you make these connections and build Relationship Capital via authentic interactions.

For instance, I had built up Relationship Capital with Barry over my entire life. Through him, I can "buy" access to top CEOs and decision-makers of huge corporations and immediately secure a six-figure contract. Through my Relationship Capital with Pat, another childhood friend, I connected with Neil Patel. Through my new connection with Neil, more 6-figure contracts have been secured. From beginning to end, I've made millions of dollars, built a successful company, and had lots of fun --> all from Relationship Capital I developed over the years.

The stronger your degree and level of Relationship Capital, the stronger your chain. The stronger your chain, the stronger your long-term prospects and potential for long-term success. You can get massive success right away and build from there. All the while, you're continuing to nurture Relationship Capital whenever and with whomever, you can.

Win-Win-Win-Win

All of this came about because I had enough on deposit with Barry to make that "withdrawal" and ask for the introductions to CEOs. I had enough on deposit with Pat to get the connection with Neil. I led with value for Neil, so I could build Relationship Capital with him and literally made a deposit. Neil was taking the biggest risk, I think, even though I guaranteed income for him whether or not we succeeded. He was risking his reputation for an upstart who couldn't turn on his computer. Fortunately, Neil saw something in me that was different. He didn't need me to know computers because he did. What I did know were relationships. All successful people trade in the game of relationships; in the end, everyone wins.

Ultimately, whenever you can create win-win transactions, you're golden. If you can create a situation where the other person or company wins by interacting with you, you're building Relationship Capital. In this particular illustration, it was a win-win-win-win transaction. Barry won because I led with value and brought more revenue his way. Neil wins because he gets more exposure and more revenue. I win because I get more connections, Relationship Capital, and money. Even better? The client wins because they received value via increased revenues from the digital marketing campaign.

We all have Relationship Capital, and we can all offer our Relationship Capital to help others, increasing our Relationship Capital. I had Relationship Capital that Barry didn't have, and he certainly had Relationship Capital that I didn't have. It's not something that was engineered, constructed, or even strategized. If I had gone into my relationships with Barry, Pat, and Neil with some determined strategy, I wouldn't have been able to develop a genuine relationship with any of them. The key is to lead with value all the time. Don't strategize why you're connecting with someone or whether or not they can help you with "this or that." Make the connection, nurture the relationship, and be friends. Make deposits to your Relationship Capital account with other people. At some point, something will come out of nothing. In other words, something organic will happen that will open doors for you and help you buy access.

Instead of manipulating situations and looking for contacts who you think can help you, make those connections and see where they go. Look for opportunities for how you can help and provide value for others, and then work backward from there. You almost reverse engineer it. You'll have these connections, these relationships, and you'll see (sometimes suddenly) how you can connect the dots for yourself and each other.

If, on the other hand, you lead with a "sale" or an "opportunity" for the other person, you're creating distance and disconnections. We have enough commercials in our lives, and I hate getting contacted by someone on social media with a "pitch." Instead, just offer a cup of coffee with me, and we can talk and see how we can help each other. That's how to get my attention and take the first step to building Relationship Capital with anyone. That's how you "buy" access with Relationship Capital.

It's all about your connections and making great first impressions.

Pat Flynn

What does relationship capital mean to you, and how has it helped you in your life?

Relationship capital is all about how connected you are. Every relationship you have can become an asset in one way or another, and the more relationship capital you own, the more opportunities are present – for you to both help others and others to help you. It's not just a name and number in a rolodex; it's a genuine connection kept over time.

Would you rather have $1,000,000 in cash or know 1,000 people very well?

I'd rather know 1,000 people very well. Because those 1,000 people may know others, and thus my connections are, in fact, more than just those 1,000 alone. And any one of those people could potentially turn into an opportunity that could gain much more over time than what one might be able to gain from 1,000,000 in cash now, for me, at least at this moment in my life.

Describe your relationship with Jeff Fenster.

Jeff and I went to middle school and high school together. We were always friendly with each other and knew a lot of the same friends, but we weren't super close. After the age of 30, however, Jeff and I reconnected on Facebook and have since had meals together talked business and family together, and I personally consider Jeff not only a dear friend but an inspiration when I look at what he's done with Everbowl and how he keeps leveling up.

Build Your Relationship Capital

What skills do you lack that could benefit your growth?

_____

_____

_____

_____

_____

Who in your network has those skills?

_____

_____

_____

_____

_____

"We must reach out our hand in friendship and dignity both to those who would befriend us and those who would be our enemy."

Arthur Ashe

Chapter 6

Be More Interested Than Interesting

Imagine you're on a first date. The person across from you makes eye contact, smiles, asks questions, and listens. After some time, you start really enjoying this date that you might have been dreading. "They're really nice," you think to yourself. "Maybe this could go somewhere."

Now, imagine the type of first date where the other person is just babbling on about themselves, everything, and nothing. Then, when they finally do take a breath and ask you something about yourself, they quickly turn the conversation back to themselves. Next, you start getting bored, then frustrated. Finally, you end the date knowing you never want to see them again.

Most of us love talking about ourselves. We're almost hardwired to do this to let others know where we might fit into their tribe. But, in truth, we often do it out of insecurity or discomfort with silence. Some of us also are afraid of making ourselves vulnerable, and revealing too much about ourselves, so we end up talking endlessly about nothing. Still, others are so self-absorbed that they want to ensure everyone knows how amazing they are.

This applies in business as well, and it certainly applies to our discussion about Relationship Capital. If you make yourself interested versus always trying to be interesting, you'll find that you'll make more meaningful connections. It's just a matter of asking questions, listening, and asking follow-up questions when needed. It's paying attention to the other person's dreams, passions, and interests.

The other person could be a first date, but it can also be a long-lost friend. Or perhaps it's someone you've known for years and is reconnecting with. The other person could be a potential client or someone who sends you lots of business. It could be your husband or wife or a dear friend. It doesn't matter. Although this book is written from the perspective of Relationship Capital related to business success, I know these ideas go much further.

Listening

We've already established how people love to talk about themselves – I know I do! Maybe you do, too. Most of us do. So, what I like to do and encourage you to try is to use that psychology to get to know someone.

When we ask questions and truly listen, we allow people to talk about themselves. What we get out of it is understanding and getting to know someone. For example, if you ask someone about their history, you might get a great story and learn a lot about them. If you follow up with a related question, it shows that you were listening and are interested.

Think of the best interviews you've seen or heard on television or in a podcast. Usually, you enjoy them because the interviewer or host is asking great questions, listening, and then asking the all-important follow-up question. "Why did you make the decision to close that business? What was going on there?"

You can understand the other person more deeply in those questions and the follow-up. When you understand someone, you can see how you can help them and give something that will build your Relationship Capital account with them. Again, not out of a goal to get something back from them, but just getting to know them and understanding how you can lead with value and do something nice for someone.

If you and I were having coffee, I might ask you questions like:

"What do you do?
"Who do you do it with?"
"What are your pain points?"
"What are you working on?"
"What are your interests and passions?"
"What are your fears?"
"What's holding you back?"
"Is there a problem that needs solving?"

I understand where you're coming from through these questions and, more importantly, the answers. You'll notice that none of them are close-ended. In other words, your answers to these questions are not simple, "yes," "no," or "maybe." They require me to lean into the conversation and listen closely as the person who asked the question. You might also notice that none are about "What can you do for me?" They really are centered on the other person.

True Conversation

When you're in a real conversation with someone, and in that conversation to learn and to help, you are immediately building Relationship Capital.

Many years ago, when I was first getting into entrepreneurship, one of my mentors had a conversation like this with me. We talked about my business and where I was going with it.

"What's your exit strategy?" he asked.
"What do you mean?" I answered, slightly confused (I was VERY young).
"Well, you should always consider how you will exit the business. I mean, you're not going to want to do this when you're eighty, are you?"

That conversation helped me understand something I hadn't considered yet, and his asking me showed me he was interested in helping me and not just "telling me what to do." He had been listening to me. We were in true conversation, and he also gave me invaluable advice.

As I've said, these concepts can be applied to any relationship, but these questions can open doors in the business realm. Perhaps not immediately, but the deposit has been made in your Relationship Capital account with whoever you're having that conversation with. Trust me.

The Cost

When you're showing that you're interested in others and helping them make connections that will advance their career and success, you're making Relationship Capital deposits. You will receive tenfold when you invest a little time, energy, and maybe even a little money. If you take two people you know and make a connection because you see how they can help each other out, now you're building Relationship Capital with both of them.

Sometimes you'll put yourself out there to make that connection in the first place. I did this with both Neil Patel and my friend Dan Fleyshman.

Dan and I grew up in the same city and rolled in the same circles but hadn't yet connected. My mentor, Dave Meltzer, was Dan's mentor, and I asked Dave to introduce us. Since we were both entrepreneurs from San Diego and had many of the same friends, we had some things in common.

As a result of that introduction, Dan asked me to speak at one of his Elevator Nights and then invited me out to coffee the next day. As we sat down, I asked Dan a lot of questions. (To this day, we haven't really ever talked "business.") From that conversation, I learned about his charity and how they were working on creating a program to help homeless people in the community.

Dan wanted to set up drop boxes that could be situated at mosques, churches, synagogues, and community centers, where people could donate supplies, such as blankets, clothing, toiletries, and other items for homeless folks. From there, a homeless person could take whatever they needed.

I knew immediately how I could help Dan and make a deposit.

"Listen, I can have those donation boxes made for you," I said.

Dan sketched a quick concept that I took back to the office. I asked our CFO to put together a mock-up of what a box like this might look like, and we sent a file to Dan three hours after that coffee. He loved it and was blown away. I sent over a prototype for the first donation box within three days.

By asking Dan questions, listening to how I might be able to help, and being interested in his work and his charity, we were able to make that initial connection. Fast-forward, and Dan is now an investor and has connected me with other investors who have become franchisees. This is all a result of me sitting down with Dan and being interested. I truly cared about his charity and wanted to help.

That's all it takes sometimes. You make "deposits" to Relationship Capital because you want to help. You make deposits by leading with and offering value to the relationship. Then, when it comes time to ask for a withdrawal, the capital you've built is more than you'll need.

Dig Your Well Before You're Thirsty - Harvey Mackay

You'll always be thirsty if you wait until you need something to build friendships. If instead, you're always building relationships and friendships, you'll never go thirsty. Instead, you'll have opportunities present themselves to you over and over, and you'll have an incredible tribe that supports you in whatever you do.

Sean Whalen

What does relationship capital mean to you, and how has it helped you in your life?

Relationship capital is the ability to leverage relationships for growth and add value for success. Not just in business but in every area of life. Friendships with diverse people allow you to expand your personal knowledge and value base and draw on humans as needed. Friendships you can lean on in time of need but also friendships you desire to win so greatly that you add your values and skill sets for their advancement and growth. Money can be invested for business growth. It can also be given away as a charitable investment to enable another. Human capital is the ability to invest in others with their personal skill set and life experiences while simultaneously being open and amicable to receipt of another's investment into your personal "bank account."

For instance, having friends and associates of different faiths or denominations allows me to always be active in my personal relationship with the deity. As these friends share their convictions and knowledge not only through social media but with me personally, it causes me to ask deeper questions about myself and check what I truly know. I have also found a great deal of expansion in being able to ask these people questions that I may still need an answer to. Having an echo chamber where everyone you associate with is of the same foundational belief does not cause you to search indoor questions, and true growth happens when you constantly question and consistently search.

Would you rather have $1,000,000 in cash or know 1,000 people very well?

I'd rather have the cash because I already have the mindset of searching! Having that capital allows me to expand my circle even further through my own efforts in business and charity work. I've found that the more I turn inward, the more connection I make externally, so for me, that million dollars would be a tool used to dive even deeper inside, and the net result is a much larger sphere of powerful and influential friends.

Describe your relationship with Jeff Fenster.

I remember meeting Jeff for the first time in Los Angeles for a business/social meeting. A business partner of mine had recently gone into business with Jeff, and I was Staying at the same hotel where this meeting/get-together was happening and was invited to join. I had connected with Jeff on social media prior to this, but this is our first face-to-face. My experience with him was just as I would have expected, knowing the type of people I do business with and the type of people my partner associates with and does business with. The mark of a great man is his interest in others, regardless of his current status or position. As we sat and talked, Jeff Asked me numerous questions about myself, my family, and my business. He spent very little time talking about the massive success Everbowl had become, and that was the reason he and I bonded. We spoke about life and family and goals, not spreadsheets, COGS, or bottom lines. That is why he has found success in business and his investment in human capital, and that is why I not only count him as a friend and mentor but have also chosen to invest in his company and brand.

Build Your Relationship Capital

In what ways do you need to be more interested than interesting?

_____

_____

_____

_____

_____

Reflect on why it's important to be interested in others.

_____

_____

_____

_____

_____

"A friend may be waiting behind a stranger's face."

Maya Angelou

Chapter 7

Buying Opportunities with Relationship Capital

My Relationship Capital with someone like Dan Fleyshman has put me on many stages because I had expressed to my network that I was interested in more speaking opportunities. You might even be reading this book because you saw me at a speaking event. I probably told you I'm 100% in front of you because of Relationship Capital. So it should be no surprise that I'm 100% writing this book because of Relationship Capital.

Now, I didn't ask my network to give me speaking engagements. It all happened because of the Relationship Capital I built, and I became interested in putting it out there.

I've since had numerous speaking engagements offered because of the Relationship Capital that I've built over time. With Relationship Capital, you're actually creating opportunities to come to you. Going back to my friendship with the checkout clerk at the grocery store, she referred me to her brother and helped me land a massive client; there was no expectation when I befriended her. Ultimately, the incredible opportunity that resulted was "bought" with that Relationship Capital.

When you have Relationship Capital, you're top of mind with other people. It's human psychology and friendship. If your friend, for example, is a huge music fan, and their favorite artist is coming to town, you might think of them and ask them to go with you. When you've got that type of relationship, as you travel through your life and your world and make meaningful connections with those around you, you can identify opportunities for them and yourself. A lot of the time, you'll see and be exposed to opportunities that you wouldn't have noticed otherwise.

This applies on a lot of levels. You can help someone looking for a job change or a career pivot. Your network can help you open into a new region or specialty. By putting yourself out there and with a full well of Relationship Capital, more opportunities are available to you. You're buying that opportunity with your Relationship Capital.

We all have had these experiences, so how do you expand your opportunities exponentially?

It's simple. Make friends with more people. Opportunities will become much more abundant, so now you're "buying" opportunity with your Relationship Capital – a resource you wouldn't have had before applying these principles. Instead of just letting relationships fall in your lap, you realize you have to build on them all the time, every day.

We are not individuals living inside a box; we are connected, social creatures. To some extent, we all crave real connections with others. We all want to feel that we're important in our community, in our society, and in the lives of others. When we can provide that for other people, we are helping them and becoming better people. So who's the better teacher in the classroom? The one who is great at teaching math concepts but doesn't connect with his students? Or is it the teacher who is great at teaching a love of math, is very effective with teaching the concepts, and has a classroom where every student feels valued and respected?

Think about your favorite teacher. Most of the time, we think of someone with whom we feel a personal connection. We think about someone who challenged us to work harder and try things we didn't think we could accomplish. Think about your favorite boss. It's usually the same thing – it's someone who challenged us, someone who valued us. We will never forget those people.

By being this for other people and creating and building on honest and sincere Relationship Capital, we are creating more opportunities for them and us!

Our ancient societies traded in Relationship Capital. For example, you hunt, and I'll pick berries, and together we'll have a complete meal, utilizing different strengths and skills. Our mutual skills and sharing of those abilities improve our lives. The same concept applies in today's world.

I'm great at sales, and you're great at computer stuff – together, we can build a digital marketing empire, even though I need help turning my computer on. Both of us have opportunities created out of our Relationship Capital. It's not even that we "find" opportunities or that opportunities "find" us. We are CREATING opportunities via Relationship Capital.

The purpose of Relationship Capital is to find a need rather than build around it. The purpose is to build Relationship Capital via friendships and friends, and then if the need arises, the well is full, and your friends can help you. Instead of looking for opportunities, live and be and do this, and you'll find those opportunities showing up. Your Relationship Capital, in many ways, puts your life on autopilot.

Finding Common Ground

As you meet people, you need to look at them in a different way than we're often trained. Instead of determining "what can you do for me?" you're looking at a much simpler aspect of being human. Your only task is to determine if you can be friends. Can you find common ground that we all share as human beings? We have common emotions, experiences, likes, and dislikes. There's something that can connect you with anyone.

Even in this day and age of political divisiveness, where some individuals are putting themselves in a like-minded bubble, it still applies. I think that isolating yourself like this will ultimately work against you, but it does nothing to further you, those around you, or society in general. When we think that what we believe is "superior" to others around us, we're being the most judgmental of them all. Instead, we all need to find a way to put those differences aside and focus on what brings us together.

This can be quite simple - a favorite musical artist, a sports team, or a love of cars or motorcycles. We can find common ground in our passion for helping those worse off than we are. There is always common ground, even if it doesn't appear so when we first meet (and judge) someone. That's where I want you to stop yourself. If you're meeting someone and judging them based on one thing you don't like, then you're missing out on friendships and opportunities.

We all have our own personalities. I might not be into music, but maybe you're a musical savant. So, music isn't going to be our commonality. Maybe instead, it will be our love of entrepreneurship, or maybe it will be art, culture, or food. Maybe your favorite food is also Ethiopian cuisine – mine, too! "There's a new place opening on 3rd street; we should check it out for lunch."

Find your common ground with everyone you meet. Build friendships and relationships that will help you become a better person, better at your career, and a better life for yourself and those around you. By looking at people openly, you'll meet and connect with people who look and sound different from you; you'll widen your reach and learning and make it clear that you are a friend. You will meet more people and make more connections than choosing to stay in some ideological bubble. Do whatever is necessary to create opportunities with as many people as possible.

It's never too late to start this. Build on the friends that you already have and reconnect with people you have lost touch with. Make sure to lead with value and with no intention of "getting something out of" the relationship. Nurture those prior and current relationships, and build on any new relationships, making deposits in your Relationship Capital account with everyone you know.

Meeting People

You can attend networking events, but as I said, those are often a waste of time if you're looking for deep connections. You can also invest in workshops and retreats and meet like-minded people. Finally, you can just be open to meeting and getting to know people at bars, parties, get-togethers, business meetings, and heck, even at the grocery store. You never know when you'll meet someone who will change your life forever.

One of my best buddies and my roommate at the time used to own a pizza place. It was a favorite hangout of mine for both the food and the friendship. Right behind his place was a beauty school where people trained to be hairstylists and cosmetologists. He had become friends with a few of the students and asked me to go with him to meet two female students. He had a crush on one of them, and I was going to meet her friend.

We met at the mall, and I quickly connected with the girl he was most interested in. He recognized it immediately and was ok with it because they were both very interesting and fun women. He and I had a quick chat on the side and were on the same page. So, I started flirting with my future wife. (Come to find out later that my wife's friend was very interested in Zach, so it all worked out perfectly!)

That meeting came from the relationship capital I had with my friend. I wasn't out looking or searching for an incredible woman to come into my life. The opportunity arose because I was trying to connect and make friends with as many people as possible.

Most people meet other people through friends, established trust networks, and a common tribe. As you build your established trust network through your relationship capital, many opportunities will be created, and your life will take on new directions.

Kent Clothier

What does relationship capital mean to you, and how has it helped you in your life?

You are a product of who you surround yourself with. This was a hard lesson for me to learn early in my career. But once I clearly understood that relationships are EVERYTHING in life and business, my career and, ultimately, my life took off. I invest heavily in nurturing my relationships. I am thoughtful and deliberate with my time. I approach people with the intent of helping them to achieve their goals, expecting nothing in return but clearly understanding that this person can bring value to my life as well. I now know that almost anything that I could want or dream of is simply a phone call or meeting away because of the time that I've invested into very specific relationships. Relationship capital = relationship leverage. That leverage point is massive and cannot be overestimated.

Would you rather have $1,000,000 in cash or know 1,000 people very well?

As would almost everyone in my inner circle - give me 1,000 quality people EVERY TIME. With those relationships - partnered with my knowledge, experience, values, faith, and work ethic - the $1,000,000 is peanuts.

Describe your relationship with Jeff Fenster.

Jeff and I met several years ago before Everbowl. We were trying to do some business together in a different industry through mutual connections. Even then, Jeff was a savvy business guy - always hustling and making big moves. Fast forward about 5 years, and I kept hearing this buzz about Everbowl here in San Diego and quickly realized it was Jeff making more moves. We quickly reconnected, and I've been an admirer ever since. We've spent some time reconnecting and now have mutual business partners and a ton of peers in common. Jeff's appeared on my podcast, and as I said, I love watching his growth and development - it's been very inspiring.

Build Your Relationship Capital

Reflect on the opportunities you've gained through your Relationship Capital.

_____

_____

_____

_____

_____

How can you provide more opportunities for others?

_____

_____

_____

_____

_____

"We need old friends to help us grow old and new friends to help us stay young."

Letty Cottin Pogrebin

Chapter 8

Buying Time with Relationship Capital

"Time is more valuable than money. You can get more money, but you can't get more time."

Jim Rohn

This is a quote I refer to in my course on Relationship Capital. When you think about it and allow it to sink in, you realize that time allows you more time for growth. For example, one of my businesses is a construction company that builds restaurants.

Just like computers, I know nothing about construction – nothing. But, through my Relationship Capital, I knew many people who were really good at construction. Moreover, they were very sophisticated and smart, so rather than trying to learn all the tools I needed to succeed in this business, my Relationship Capital allowed me to save that time by connecting with people who already knew what they were doing.

Because they already knew what they were doing, and I didn't have much to manage, it allowed me to build that company and build on other efforts much faster. I saved time, not just in the startup and launch of the company, but in other aspects. My relationships were bringing in the right people and resources. I was also able to bring in the right investors because I knew the right investors. I basically act as the general manager of the whole shebang and let people do what they already know how to do. I stay out of their way, saving their time and mine.

Concentrating Your Time

Years of doing business are an asset. If you've been doing what you're doing for five years, ten years, or more, there's validity to you and your efforts. You have built-in credibility because you've given time to your craft or enterprise. Unfortunately, there's no real shortcut to time –

you can't buy ten years of experience. With Relationship Capital, however, you can accelerate the process. Let me explain.

You may not have or want ten years in any business or enterprise. With Relationship Capital, you can tap into the time that others have spent in the enterprise or field. I know one serial entrepreneur who's brilliant at buying companies that have already established themselves. He can identify those with potential and who have already made their mark in the community or the field. He finds these opportunities through his connections and through his network. That's right – his Relationship Capital.

Even though he might have just a year in the business, the company has been around for ten years, or the manager has been doing this for 20 years. As long as he lets the pros do their job and gives them the financial resources they need to improve their revenue, he's golden. Ultimately, his Relationship Capital accelerates his "time" in the business.

Time as a Limited Asset

We like to think of time as limitless, but we all know it's not true. For example, how many of us have taken a three-week vacation, thinking that will surely be enough time to relax and unwind, but at the end of those three weeks, we want just one more week. If we had booked that vacation for a month, we would still probably want one more week.

Time is very limited. No one gets out of this life alive. We all have a limited timeframe in which to live and be happy. And, as I talked about, there's no shortcut to time. We can't make a year go faster or slower. We can't skip a week we don't like and jump to the next. Time, even though it's a human construct, is limited by its very definition and by our own mortality.

With that said, you can accelerate your life within the time you have. You can make the most of life by doing more in a day, a week, or a month than you would have. You can make connections and build relationships that bring you "shortcuts" in the sense of accelerating your progress. You can move through time like a time traveler when you have Relationship Capital with people who can help you surf time. Surround yourself with people smarter than you who can teach you how to do something, and make sure you pay them forward. Lead with value to get value in the future. Time won't stand still for you, but you can make time work better with Relationship Capital.

Of course, I wanted access to Aaron's knowledge and was willing to pay for access to his experience. I wanted to pick up the phone and say, "Hey, we're thinking about doing this… what are your thoughts?" I wanted to know what we could do to build a world-class franchise offering and become excellent at what we do. With Aaron's expertise, we could achieve that in a very short time. I wasn't going to ask for that access and offer him nothing while, in the meantime, making money off what was shared. Hence, the offer for equity. Just as you've seen on programs like *Shark Tank*, that was an investment of money well worth it for me and time well worth it for Aaron.

What comes around, goes around, and time is the same way. So even though it may seem like it's passing you by, and you have no control over it (which is literally true), you have control over how you use it. This doesn't mean you spin around like a personal cyclone (a la *Looney Tunes'* Tasmanian Devil). That's working hard and not working smart.

Instead, be open to making friends, and building those relationships, so you can take a side road that you didn't see on the map or have someone direct you to a faster route to your goal. You can utilize and tap into the Relationship Capital you build to buy time and exponentially grow and achieve your goals. Good people do good business, and friends don't screw each other. Friendships create Relationship Capital and opportunity and accelerate time. Gain recognizes gain, and we recognize who is good at what they do. Surround yourself with those people and build that tribe and team. Build on your Relationship Capital, leading with value first for each other, and before you know it, you're years ahead of where you would be otherwise.

John Lee Dumas

What does relationship capital mean to you, and how has it helped you in your life?

In eight years, I've interviewed over 26,000 successful entrepreneurs for my podcast *Entrepreneurs on Fire*. When I wrote my book, I reached out to these connections for help, and they were happy to give it. Building good relationships is a tool for success.

Would you rather have $1,000,000 in cash or know 1,000 people very well?

I prefer cash. The reason – knowing 1,000 people well doesn't necessarily mean those are 1,000 people I would want to know well or want to be surrounded by. I'm a firm believer that you are the average of the 5 people you spend the most time with. With the money, I'd have more opportunities to build meaningful relationships with a much larger sum of people. Whether that be 5, 10, or 100, I would be able to devote more resources and time to those that add value to my life.

Describe your relationship with Jeff Fenster.

Jeff Fenster appeared on my podcast, and I've always been impressed with the knowledge and value he's shared with the world.

Build Your Relationship Capital

How do you spend your time?

_____

_____

_____

_____

_____

How can you take advantage of it more?

_____

_____

_____

_____

_____

"Right now, someone you haven't met is out there wondering what it would be like to meet someone like you."

Unknown

Chapter 9

Relationship Capital Buys Credibility

Through my relationship with an investor for Everbowl, I was able to make a connection with the head of gift cards at Costco. I was excited about this prospect since, obviously, having your company's name in Costco is great brand exposure and marketing. If we could get gift cards for Everbowl in Costco, we would also bring in more revenue and probably introduce Everbowl to new customers.

Here's where Relationship Capital can be used to lead you to another tactic. Since I had no direct connections at Costco, and my investor's connection was not as strong as other connections, I had to utilize another strategy. I call it pleasantly persistent, whereas other people call it a pain in the ass!

Basically, what I'm doing here is building on the Relationship Capital to get an introduction, or even just a name and number, and taking it from there. Sometimes Relationship Capital doesn't get you the touchdown, but it can get you possession of the ball or give you great field position, like a solid punt return. It can get you in the door, so to speak, so that you at least have a shot. It won't close the deal per se, but without Relationship Capital, you don't even get the name or phone number.

So, for this effort, I set a reminder on my phone to call Costco every Friday. Again, I'd be pleasant, not pushy, but persistent. It would sound something like this:

"Hey Joe, it's Jeff from Everbowl. Just wondering if today's the day we can get Everbowl into Costco. Is there anything we need to do to get this done?"

Most of the time, the response was slightly cold. *"Hey Jeff, I think you called me last week and the week before. You really don't need to call me every week, you know. You're not big enough, and we're not ready yet."*

"Hey, I totally understand, Joe. I'm not trying to be a pain in the ass. I'm trying to be pleasantly persistent and demonstrate my commitment to the cause. I want to make sure you know

that when the time is right, we really want this. It means so much that I just want to check in once a week and ensure we stay in touch."

After a bit more chit-chat, if given that much time, I would close the conversation with, *"Well, hey, you have a great weekend, and I hope you're doing something fun. Hope you had a great week, and I look forward to talking with you next week."*

I would sometimes state, *"Hey, I know it might be a little annoying, but I don't want there to be a time when the opportunity opens, and I'm not there, first in line."*

So, if you evaluated it on its face value, the initial introduction didn't produce anything. If you were betting on Relationship Capital alone to get you certain deals, connections, and closes, you'd think this one fell short. But combining my weekly phone calls with the Relationship Capital that got me Joe's name and number in the first place can lead to success. After eleven months of these weekly phone calls, we got in. So, about forty-four calls later, maybe five minutes a call, about 3.5 hours of my time over a year. Not bad.

The reason I bring this up now is two-fold. One is that Relationship Capital can and will open doors and close deals for you. Often, it just gets you on the playing field, and that's just as valuable. Once you're in the game, your hard work, consistency, persistence, and pleasantness (building Relationship Capital) gets you the touchdown.

Credibility

Once we were in the Costco system, now we had major credibility behind our name and brand. It's not so much the Relationship Capital that we might have with any individual at Costco, but the relationship we have with capital. Once we have that relationship in place and can show evidence of it through the gift cards available in x number of stores, we carry more weight and credibility when we look for our next partnership.

I'm convinced that we got that first gift card deal with Costco because the powers that be realized how dedicated we were and how important this was to us. Of course, they would only make decisions that can benefit their bottom line, but those decisions are always risky. Having the belief that we would stand behind their decision and do them proud, I think, is part of the process of choosing who to offer gift cards for.

So, we also built Relationship Capital with individuals at Costco, and that Relationship Capital then came into play as we looked to grow and expand our brand. Eventually, we're not appearing to be "small beans" anymore. We're in Costco after eleven months of phone calls. After eleven months of "nagging." We made it into a powerful retail setting. We've got some street cred now. The credibility that we wouldn't have otherwise.

Because Costco is such a big name, it was almost like having a celebrity endorsement. From Costco, I wanted to get into Petco Park in San Diego (the Padre's stadium). I used the same tactic and called them, and they said, "No." I patiently persisted, called around, and got to the right people when I was told they had already decided on their food vendors for the year. "No problem," I responded. Every Friday, I would still call. This time, though, I could mention our relationship with Costco, our number of franchises, our popularity, etc. Finally, after a few months of this, I connected with the decision-maker. He stated that he had heard of my weekly calls and that he should speak with me. I told him about our brand and how I loved that they brought in local food. I shared that we were a local chain; I am a die-hard Padres fan from San Diego and would love to be a part of the team. Then, of course, I mentioned our gift cards were in Costco. "Oh? They're in Costco?" his interest was piqued. The tone changed.

With that validation from Costco, I could use that Relationship Capital to open another door at Petco Park. The credibility of our relationship with Costco showed the folks at Petco Park that we were a real brand, would stick around, and weren't just a fly-by-night vendor.

That got us a face-to-face meeting that eventually got us into Petco Park. Finally, we had the credibility and now the audience to show what we did and how we could add to the food vendor team at Petco Park. That initial Relationship Capital with the investor got us (after several phone calls) Relationship Capital with Costco, which then started our building Relationship Capital with the San Diego Padres.

Funny sidenote… when we got the deal with the park, they said, "Ok, it takes a season to build out your space, so we'll get you in next year." I told them I could finish it in two weeks since we had built our own restaurants. They thought that was cute, but I insisted they show me the space, and we were up and running within the month. This built even more Relationship Capital because they saw what we could do and are talking to us about helping them build other stands.

Accelerating Credibility

Make no mistake. You build brand integrity and credibility by offering a great product or service and backing it up. You can create your own credibility by being around for a few years and making it through tough and easier economic times. Like anything else, there's no shortcut. I can't "buy" credibility by putting out a whole bunch of advertising and hanging up a sign. It's built over time and over very hard work. Once you get one company or individual to believe in you, you

110

gain more and more credibility. You're at the table, and you get more connections if you're good at what you do. Everbowl is now in Macy's, Vegas, and other Western stadiums.

As with everything else that Relationship Capital affords, credibility can be built faster, more efficiently, and more effectively with Relationship Capital.

Let's go back to our football game analogy. If you have a great punt return (Relationship Capital) but fumble the ball the next play, you're back at square one or even worse. However, if you take advantage of that punt return and play smart, quickly, and effectively, you get your touchdown. Rarely it's with one deep throw down the field; usually, it's a battle on the ground, with pushing, shoving, and bruises. But, if you persist, demonstrate great sportsmanship, and play smart, you cross into the end zone. You've won a game, and it's on to the Superbowl.

Credibilities, like anything else in business and life, are hard-earned. Just remember that Relationship Capital can grease the wheels for you and help things go smoother and faster. It's part of the game, making it more fun to play and watch.

Roland Frasier

What does relationship capital mean to you, and how has it helped you in your life?

Relationship capital is the invisible value built through networking. Here each relationship acts like a bank account into which you make deposits by providing value to that relationship. As you do that, it builds its own equity capital.

Later you can withdraw and tap that equity to receive value for yourself in the form of favors, connections, investments, advice, partnerships, etc.

This is why there is a saying that your network equals your net worth.

Would you rather have $1,000,000 in cash or know 1,000 people very well?

If the 1k people are people I chose and curated the relationships with, then the 1k people. So, I'd take the $1M and use half of it to create 1k extremely valuable relationships if it is random people.

Describe your relationship with Jeff Fenster.

I met Jeff through a business partner named Ryan Deiss. Jeff and I made an effort to stay in touch over the years, each helping the other, and eventually, we were able to do business together. With any luck, we will continue to find more opportunities to connect one another to other valuable resources and relationships and do many more business deals together. Oh, also, Jeff is a cool, sincere, genuinely authentic human, so he is also a friend!

Build Your Relationship Capital

Reflect on your current credibility.

_____

_____

_____

_____

_____

How can you improve it?

_____

_____

_____

_____

_____

"Strangers are just friends waiting to happen."

Rod McKuen

Chapter 10

Developing Relationship Capital

As I've already discussed, the fundamental basis of Relationship Capital is recognizing that every single person you meet is an opportunity. Every. Single. Person. I'm reminded, again, of the grocery store friend who got me that huge contract for my payroll company, which developed into even more contracts and connections. Everybody can help you, and you can help everyone that you meet.

In this chapter, I want to talk about some key steps you can take to start developing Relationship Capital in your life. Remember, this doesn't happen overnight. If you expect to read this book and then be able to use Relationship Capital in your life immediately, you've missed the point. When you go into a relationship thinking they can help advance you somehow, you're diverging from what I've been saying here. You're trying to take a shortcut and manipulate Relationship Capital, but by its very definition, it can't be manipulated. Once you're in that realm, you're just "networking" in that way that I hate. You need to consistently build real and true relationships.

So, how do you do that? Let's look at some ideas:

- **Say "Hello" to Three Strangers Today**

This is a no-brainer. Your next best friend is a stranger to you now. If you take the initiative to be friendly, you might make a nice connection that can last a lifetime, and at some point, you might find yourselves in a position to help each other out. Win-win. I've heard stories of people meeting on Facebook, in a shared interest group, and becoming lifelong friends. Maybe you know someone who met their life partner in a chance meeting at the park. Especially if you know you have something in common like you're at a dog park, striking up conversations with strangers there can develop into a nice relationship, and make deposits in your Relationship Capital account.

116

- **Connect with Acquaintances**

Get into a deeper conversation with three acquaintances you know but haven't really invested any time into at this point. Maybe you say "hi" to a neighbor every day. Perhaps, on your way to work, when you pick up the paper, you see the same clerk at the convenience store or newspaper stand. Maybe you're at a conference and see someone you briefly met a few months ago. How about the parents of your kids' friends? There are dozens and dozens of acquaintances you have that you can chat with and spend more time getting to know them. Be genuine. Be real. Make connections with acquaintances.

- **Pleasantly Persistent**

We've talked about this one already, and I can't overemphasize how effective this technique is. It demonstrates your commitment to a process or relationship, and you can build Relationship Capital out of it. If it's done right, it can become a friendly exchange, where you are getting to know the other person, and they're getting to know you. If you're 100% friendly and kind 100% of the time, you'll inevitably win them over. Even if it doesn't result in the transaction, you thought it might, it may very well turn into a connection that introduces you to another opportunity you would never have known about.

117

- **Meet for Coffee or Lunch**

Take some time and have coffee with a business associate or connection, or have lunch with someone who does work that you're interested in. For example, a good friend, Scott, used to work with the Padres. This was when I was talking with them about getting something set up for Everbowl. We bumped into each other at a local farmer's market and struck up a conversation. I invited him to lunch, which eventually turned into our friendship. Was I interested in meeting and getting to know him because he was with the Padres? Sure. But also, I wanted to make a real, genuine connection. Scott's no longer with the Padres, and our friendship continues.

- **Have Fun**

I can't take credit for this next idea, but it's perfect for this point. When working for the payroll services company, I would take Payday candy bars to potential clients… on Payday. "It's Payday – here are your Payday bars!" This became a relatively regular routine, resulting in friendships and connections with gatekeepers to the gatekeeper. In addition, I would engage in sincerely interested conversations, which occasionally would result in an exception.

- **Create "Exceptions"**

When you can build Relationship Capital just by being friendly, sometimes one of your connections will make an exception for you. This happened with the Payday candy, for example. After a few months of dropping by, chatting, and being interested, I'd always say something like, *"Well, let me know if we can help you with payroll. I really do think we have the best services for the dollar."*
"I usually can't do this but let me make an exception for you and get you on Linda's calendar next week."
I had created an "exception."

- **Authentic Contacts**

I mentioned it earlier, but it really irks me when I get a connection request from someone on LinkedIn or Instagram that's just a commercial. There's no sincerity, and it's obvious that the other person wants something from me. At least several times a week, I'll get a contact request that goes something like this:

"Hey, big fan of yours. Would love to connect!"
Now, I love making connections, so I always respond, *"Sure, let's connect."*
What pisses me off is when they write back, *"Great…what do you do?"*

119

Ha! Now I know you aren't a fan, and you're not interested in doing any work with me. But you certainly aren't leading with value. You haven't even done your homework to the point of knowing what I do for a living when it's all laid out on my profile. Lazy.

- **Do Your Homework**

It doesn't take long to get information on someone or something you're interested in. For example, let's say that a LinkedIn individual did just a little bit of research on me. It would take five minutes to learn about Everbowl and the digital marketing projects I'm working on. You'd also quickly learn about my workshops on Relationship Capital and get a feel for what I teach on LinkedIn. From there, you could quickly send a note, *"Hey, I'm a big fan. I would love to ask you some questions about how Relationship Capital can work in long-distance connections across the country. Can we meet for coffee sometime soon?"*

Not everyone will say yes to this request, but you've gotten the conversation started and shown that you did your homework.

- **Fill Your Bucket - One Drop at a Time**

Too often, we see the world and people for what can fill our bucket instantly. We look for the one thing that will bring us *x, y,* or *z.* I see this also when people are trying to figure out budgets and how to save money. They look for the one thing that will save them $3,000 a month instead of looking for the ten things that will save them $300 a month on average. Friendships and Relationship Capital are this way, too. On any given day, you could have interactions with twenty strangers. It could be the woman who took your order at the café or the man who pointed to the fastest lane in the grocery store. It could be the bus station attendant you see every time you fill up your car or the mail delivery person covering your neighborhood. Each person represents a drop of water that can eventually fill your bucket. Unfortunately, very rarely can we fill this bucket with an open tap? More often, it's a slow drip that, when we're patient, results in more meaningful and plentiful Relationship Capital opportunities.

- **Develop Your People Skills**

I've always been the type of person who could talk to strangers comfortably. I'm great in sales because I'm very comfortable chatting people up and making that connection, but not all of us are. Some of us, like with any skill, need to practice. There are many ways of doing this, and if you go into it with no agenda or specific intention – say to make friends – it can be easier. If, on the other hand, you're expecting some

121

specific response, you can get more nervous, and that "intention" can be sensed by the other person.

There are many techniques for improving your ability to connect with other people. The important thing is to practice, practice, and practice some more. Practice until you become more comfortable with it, and it becomes second nature. Reach out, especially when you don't feel comfortable, with no other purpose or goal but to make a connection, no matter how brief.

- **A Little Story**

I love this story, so I must share it here. When we talk about meeting people casually, who end up rocking your world, I think of Eric. He does all our amazing branding for Everbowl, even coming up with the name (which is WAY better than my original idea). We met because my eight-year-old daughter had a crush on a boy from her soccer practice. Yup, you guessed it, Eric is that little boy's dad. We kicked off a great friendship and now have a fantastic working relationship.

Where you find your next friend or friends who can really help you in your life and you help them in theirs can be anywhere. At work, your kids' school, the gym, the train, and the park. Anywhere. Your job is to develop those connections and keep your heart and mind open to the possibilities of current and future opportunities.

Cody Sperber (Clever Investor)

What does relationship capital mean to you, and how has it helped you?

The power of proximity principle and networking, hiring mentors, surrounding myself with successful people, and serving as a way of breaking into powerful groups have been major keys to my success.

Every next level starts with a relationship and exposure to that level's principles. Without that exposure and influence, I would never have achieved the level of success I currently have or will have.

Would you rather have $1,000,000 in cash or know 1,000 people very well?

That's a tough one because I am an investor and could easily turn that Million into many more...but for the sake of this conversation, those relationships could easily turn into a lifetime of amazing adventures and profitable relationships, so I'll go with knowing 1000 REALLY WELL because I know how to capitalize on those relationships.

Describe your relationship with Jeff Fenster.

Simple...I connected with Jeff through a mutual relationship with Dan Fleyshman and, from day one, was impressed with Jeff's attitude towards the companies he creates. His love of the product, the customer experience, and the way he creates FOR PURPOSE companies are not only admirable...but exciting to watch at the same time.

I know I could rely on Jeff for help, advice, or a warm introduction, and he would do it without hesitation... that's just the kind of guy he is!

Build Your Relationship Capital

How can you show the people in your life that you care more, thus building a better relationship?

_____

_____

_____

_____

_____

How can you do the same with strangers, opening new doorways?

_____

_____

_____

_____

_____

"Go out into the world today and love the people you meet. Let your presence light new light in the hearts of others."

Mother Teresa

Chapter 11

More on Dig the Well Before You Get Thirsty

More than 80% of jobs are found with warm or "pseudo-warm" introductions, as Jordan Harbinger reports in his class, "The Art of Networking." On the other hand, only 3% are found by sending a resume to someone you don't know. By building relationships before you need anything, you're always ready for whatever is thrown your way. For example, if you wait to network with real estate professionals AFTER becoming a realtor, you'll be six to twelve months without genuine leads or relationships. On the other hand, if you dig that well all the time, you'll have immediate leads and network opportunities.

When you have enough friends, it doesn't matter what you do in your career. For example, you must let your network know if you're doing online marketing for a while and then shift to real estate. Then, your friends will take care of you. There will be little to no "introductory" phase to your new pathway. Instead, your network of friends and connections will know, trust you, like you, and send you more references.

If you wait until a chance to start "making friends," you're far behind the curveball, and you'll struggle more than you need to. When you've built up Relationship Capital without any specific need for it, just by being a friend and a good person, any transitions or shifts you make in your life will be more successful and smoother. Whatever industry you end up going toward, your Relationship Capital will help you achieve success quickly – that's building the well before you're thirsty.

Don't Wait Until You Need It

The best time to start this technique of building your Relationship Capital was twenty years ago, but we can't turn back time. The second-best time to start is now, and I mean today. Review the ideas in the previous chapter to get going. If you live in a community that isn't exactly filled with "movers and shakers," or you just don't know that many, much of this can be accomplished online. It's never been easier to connect with people. Begin now to build up these connections; even if you're comfortable exactly where you are in life, don't wait to do this.

Go online and find an influencer that you admire in your field. Better yet, find five or ten. Take some time to review the content they've posted and make thoughtful comments. Not just a "this is great" type of comment. Do your homework (see the previous chapter), and comment with some substance:

"I love your thoughts on network marketing. Would love to hear your ideas on how to do so in today's virtual world! Thanks for the great content!"

For each influencer your comment with, chances are you'll hear back from a few. Keep doing this. Keep connecting with someone you don't know yet. Start digging that well so you can fill it up with buckets and buckets of friends and connections you're creating. This is not for manipulative purposes but to make real, meaningful connections. As you start and continue these conversations via comments on content, you'll begin to build a relationship with that person. At some point, you can send a personal message. Most people are accessible these days, and you can pretty much get in touch with just about anyone. Of course, there are exceptions, but it's not like you will immediately make a one-on-one connection with the Michael Jordans of the world. You can, however, make immediate connections with people who might be able to help you someday.

The power of social media means you can tweet The Rock and the President of the United States. This means you can absolutely tweet the state head of the real estate board or send a private message to the head of the local chamber of commerce. You can develop meaningful relationships with all these people. Don't forget that everyone can become a friend and contact who can help you down the line, if you're leading with value and never on a take-take-take path.

Look in Your Community

Most business transactions and connections are on a local community level. You can start meeting people in your community instantly. Again, look at some of the ideas I outlined in the previous chapter. Going deeper into a conversation with an acquaintance or starting a conversation with a stranger, you'll never know where it might go. Even if you don't make a personal connection with an individual, they might see you again and say, "Hey there!" They might know someone who just met you, and they can say, "Oh, that guy, yeah, he seems nice. He always says 'Hi' and chats with me a little every time he comes into the store."

You'd be surprised where "small talk" can lead you. We can find common ground, mutual interests, and passions through small talk. Most people can find some type of commonality with most other people. There are always connections to be made. The other day, I was walking my dog in my new neighborhood when an older woman passed by in her car and said, "I saw you jogging here the other day. Do you live here?" I told her I had just bought the house down the street, so we continued to chat and found a common interest in flying. Long story short, we were invited to a barbecue at our new neighbor's home. I don't know if this will benefit me or our business, but that's not the point. I've made a new connection and friend by having a friendly conversation with a stranger. We'll see what happens. One of my favorite mentors once said, "Something will happen."

Be Yourself

When they meet or see me at a workshop, many assume I've always been gregarious and outgoing. They think it's always been easy for me to start conversations with strangers, but I haven't always been this way. My natural state is to be very shy. This Relationship Capital strategy works for me because I like authenticity and love sitting across from someone at a café and getting to know them. Even when I am having a conversation with a stranger, I'm myself. I also know

131

that that "stranger" will help me dig and fill my well before I ever need anything from them or anyone for that matter.

Whoever you are, whatever your core personality, if you can show that to the people around you and show them that you respect them and their time, opinion, perspective, and life experience, you'll overcome any "flaws" that you think you might have. Today, we are very politically divided, but I think we always have been. It's just that politics are so "in your face" these days that long gone are the days when our parents quietly cast their votes and went home. Our culture and society have changed.

You don't have to hide your politics, nor do you have to have them posted on your forehead. All perspectives are valid, and if we listen to and respect each other, we can always find common ground. It's important and critical to be ourselves, show ourselves, and respect those around us.

Where you place yourself, literally and figuratively, allows you to be your truer self. I like the café setting because I can be myself, converse with you, and find some shared interest or common ground. For me, a "networking event" is to Relationship Capital as bars are to dating. It just feels fake. Everyone has an agenda. No one can be real. So, if you put yourself in places where it's easy for people to be themselves and you to be yourself, you're more likely to make a real connection with someone. That's why "natural habitats," like taking a walk in the neighborhood with your dog or going grocery shopping, are a better setting for you to be yourself.

Genuine Wins

The bottom line is that you'll draw genuine people into your life if you're genuine. You'll find yourself making friends. You'll be digging the well before you need to draw from it. People will want to be around you, and you'll want to help each other out. That's why I say, over and over, that I love making friends – it's one of my core values. It helps me make connections that feed my soul and help me on my adventures.

The most interesting people have fans – the most interested people have relationships.

Bobby Castro

What does relationship capital mean to you, and how has it helped you?

It was everything to where I am today in my life financially. Spiritually, family, marriage, father, and grandfather.

Would you rather have $1,000,000 in cash or know 1,000 people well?

People all day long and more so the right people.

Describe your relationship with Jeff Fenster.

Jeff reminds me of myself a lot as he is one that truly understands Human Capital and the importance of relationships. I decided to invest with Jeff due to his core values of long-term thinking and being completely hands-on in the mud with his employees. In addition, I enjoy his humble ways of being a sponge as to how to scale and crew at the massive value of business.

Build Your Relationship Capital

How do you usually approach people, start conversations, and initiate friendships?

_____

_____

_____

_____

_____

How can you be more yourself and give people a comfortable space to do the same?

_____

_____

_____

_____

_____

"I love meeting new people; everyone has a story to tell. We should all listen sometimes."

Kim Smith

Chapter 12

Check Your Ego at the Door

You could subtitle this chapter "The Importance of Authenticity," which I've talked about extensively in this book. What I'm reminded of repeatedly is how important it is to leave behind your ego, especially when meeting new people.

If you're at an event and have casual conversations with fifty people, asking them questions about themselves, those fifty people will think about you as a "nice guy" or "nice woman." They'll probably also think of you as "interesting," even though you hardly said anything about yourself. If you engage in those conversations and listen more than you talk, you will automatically build Relationship Capital directly or indirectly.

You might have heard the saying (I'm paraphrasing) that if you want to appear to be a genius, keep your mouth shut. I think this is true. Think about it, if you're in a conversation with a small group and don't know much about the topic. Still, you nod and ask inquisitive questions such as, "Why do you think that?" or "What evidence have you seen on that?" you'll seem super intelligent. In a way, you are because you're actively listening and learning. If, on the other hand, you interrupt and push your ideas and opinions in the group, the others are likely to think one of two things… either you're an idiot, or you're full of yourself.

I can't overemphasize the importance of checking your ego at the door. This applies to all aspects of life. When you're submitting work for a client, it's not YOUR project; it's theirs. You must check your ego to ensure they're getting what they were looking and paying for. Check your ego at the door if you're meeting with an investor. The investor wants to know how it will be to work with you, and if you're abrasive and defensive, you're out. If you want to get to know someone – really know someone – you must check your ego at the door.

One of the best ways to do this is to be "anonymous."

Hidden in Plain Sight

Maybe you've seen the TV show *Undercover Boss*. Here, the CEO of a major corporation disguises themselves and gets a job working at their company, usually in a "low-level" position far below his or her pay grade. In this program, the boss gets to know the working conditions, learns about some of his/her employees, and makes real and sometimes lasting relationships with key individuals that they would have never met otherwise. (For a humorous version of this, check out Adam Driver's appearances on Saturday Night Live, where he's an Undercover Boss as the murderous Kylo Ren of the *Star Wars* series. Brilliant!)

This idea goes back to my thoughts on treating your friends like your boss and your boss like your friend. For example, when speaking to our boss as boss, we often tell them what we think they want to hear instead of telling them the truth. If, on the other hand, the other person doesn't really know what our "status" is, they can be more open and truthful.

Most of us aren't famous, so I'm not talking about that aspect. However, there's a well-known story out there where someone at a party approached one of the founders of Microsoft, Paul Allen. When asked what he did, Allen replied, "I'm in computers; what do you do?" Clearly, Allen was engaging in the building of Relationship Capital.

I often go into an Everbowl location and chit-chat with the customers about their experience. I ask them what they thought of their bowl, the concept, the service, etc. Very often, they ask me if I'm the manager. I always say, "Yes." I feel that if I do that versus telling them I'm the owner, they'll be more honest with me.

That anonymity, by choice, allows me to get to know you better and to get to know anyone I meet. Instead of showing how important I think I am, I am conveying, just through that sheer anonymity, that I'm interested in getting to know someone and understanding the situation. I think putting our ego away is the greatest way we can really give value to people and take the time to go deeper into a conversation. The other person is more likely to open up if I hold a "powerful" position, and we're much more likely to develop a true connection.

Conversation Versus an Interview

As I've discussed, our goal is to have conversations with people, to get to know them, and to find common ground. When we've put our ego aside, we ask many and even more follow-up questions. We also have to ensure it's a conversation, not an interview. You want to be doing maybe 30% of the talking and listening at least 70% of the time. At the same time, if you're simply asking question after question without inserting your ideas and input here and there, it will feel weird to the other person.

You can do this by finding that commonality and mentioning your connection. "I love entrepreneurship, too.

What a ride! What's been your experience?" What you want to avoid is changing the subject back to you; that's ego. Instead, you can bring it back to you and immediately toss it back, as above.

"I love entrepreneurship, too. What a ride!" brings the conversation to you, and
"What's been your experience?" lobs it back to your partner.

When you can do this, you'll start taking down the walls we all have when we're around people we don't know very well. This wall is expected, as we're all hardwired to keep our distance from new people since they're not a member of our "tribe" yet. So don't take it personally if you sense that wall. It can be especially tricky if you're talking to someone with little notoriety, as they're used to fake "friendships."

As you continue the conversation, you'll find more in common and something to remember about the person the next time you see them. Through the conversation, you'll pick up on cues based on their words, maybe items you see in the background during your Zoom call, or even what they're wearing.

One day, I was having a meeting outside of one of our Everbowl locations. As the manager and I were sitting there, a car pulled up. Out hops a vibrant middle-aged woman wearing super bright, glittery glasses. Now, since I like to make friends with everyone, I interrupt my conversation with the manager to say, "Those glasses are killer!" She smiled, and we chatted a bit, mostly about where she got them (at a party) and what a great day it was. When she came back out after ordering her bowl, she sat next to us.

We chatted and got great feedback about Everbowl, and she set off.

"Well, it was great meeting you, Jeff!"
"You, too – I'll always remember you because those glasses are fantastic!"
She ran back to her car, dug around a little, and brought me a pair to give me. She had some extras from the party.
"Awesome, thanks!" I said as she drove off and waved.

During the meeting that I was having with that Everbowl manager, we were talking about company culture and how we want customers to remember their experiences. So, this was a perfect example, and to this day, we have those bright blue, glittery eyeglasses in that restaurant's office to remember how to connect with our customers.

When we can break down the wall that all of us build around ourselves and get in a little deeper in conversation to get to know those around us, we all win. We are building relationships, and friendships, leading with value and making deposits in Relationship Capital. As a result, the other person feels valued, feels like they matter, and has a better day.

Chris Cole

What does relationship capital mean to you, and how has it helped you?

It's immeasurable the value of it, to be honest. Although my line of work is based on athleticism, my job isn't unlike many others regarding human interaction. First, somebody must believe in you and give you a shot. Then, you build that relationship before and after being allowed to show what you've got.

If someone can't be good in the tour van, they won't get the chance.

Would you rather have $1,000,000 in cash or know 1,000 people well?

Although a million in cash seems awesome, you're likely to burn through it without knowing the right people. Knowing 1,000 people well will give you a better chance at Making that money and potentially more while living a better life. One with meaningful relationships.

Describe your relationship with Jeff Fenster.

Jeff is a friend. Yes, he is brilliant minded with business and has achieved great success, but first and foremost, he is a wonderful friend. I also get inspired by his drive, courage, and ability.

Build Your Relationship Capital

What is your current ego like?

_____

_____

_____

_____

_____

How can you be more authentic?

_____

_____

_____

_____

_____

"Don't be afraid of new beginnings. Don't shy away from new people, energy, and surroundings. Embrace new chances at happiness."

Billy Chapata

Chapter 13

Making Deposits in Your Relationship Capital Account

Here's where you put the pedal to the metal. In this chapter, I'll briefly outline how you can make deposits, even if you think you're too busy, even if you're communicating with friends that you're out of touch with, or even if you think you're not "good enough" at this Relationship Capital thing.

I'm here to tell you that it's easy, and you have countless daily opportunities. Practically from the moment, you wake up to the moment you go to sleep. Of course, I'm exaggerating, but only just a little. Remember, these techniques are not just for business but for the quality of your personal life. In the morning, my wife draws in messages on the steamed bathroom mirror for me – these are little ways she tells me she loves me. One of the goals of Relationship Capital is to show the people we care about that they have a place in our lives. They own real estate in our minds and in our hearts.

Relationship Capital can be used to connect with people you know. But, even as easy as it is to connect in today's world, it's just as easy to lose sight of each other. When we are not making regular deposits in our accounts with friends, loved ones, and business associates, it's like our account is losing value to inflation. It's much like a savings account that only earns .3% interest, but the inflation rate is 3%. So, unless we make regular deposits and ensure our "money" gets better interest, we lose those connections.

When you're rich in relationships, you find that your quality of life is better than it otherwise would be, and your network almost feels like a security blanket. I'm not interested in fake relationships or fake friendships. I'm not out to be a "major," and I just know everybody's name. I want to know YOU. I want to get to a point where you and I can call each other in a pinch and know we'll help each other. No strings attached. Not a second thought. For example, maybe my car breaks down, it's been towed to the shop, I'm in your city, and I'll give you a call. "Man, can I crash on your couch tonight?"

Unless either of us can make that call, we're not where I want us to be.

Details

Making deposits in your Relationship Capital is all about the little details. It knows what someone's favorite band is and sends them a cool pic of their favorite artist or a funny meme that lets them know you're thinking of them. Basically, letting someone know they're important to you – and this message carries value – at some point, you may need to withdraw. By continuously making and nurturing relationships throughout your life, you can have friends that will help you through anything.

Find a way of making deposits with your time, money, resources, and/or expertise. Here are some quick ideas:

• Send a few daily texts to friends you haven't connected with lately. For example, "Hey, thinking of you; hope all is well!"
• Write quick check-in emails and texts about specific things in the person's life. For example, "How's your mom doing? Are you hanging in there? Need anything?"
• Make an introduction for a friend launching a new product, website, etc.
• For someone launching a podcast, make suggestions and connections for interviews.

- Share a friend's new product/launch on your social media stories.
- Offer to "be the customer" to help a friend struggling with sales.
- Is a friend moving? We all hate moving! Offer to help for a couple of hours. Drop off extra moving boxes and supplies. Offer to have them use your truck. Even if you're busy, you can help them out.
- Send fun memes or share articles you think they would find interesting.

There are a million ways to do this. Like I said at the beginning of the chapter, throughout the day, you have opportunities to make deposits with almost everyone you see during your travels. These are simple conversations you can have where you slowly get to know someone – really get to know someone. Thinking of my neighbor who just invited me to a barbecue, I would guess she's in her late 70s. By being open to Relationship Capital and making friends whenever and wherever possible, you get to know amazing people you wouldn't otherwise meet.

In your mind, right now, go through your day. It might look like this…

After you finish your morning work, you're having breakfast with a few friends at your favorite bagel place. On the way, you stop to get gas and go in to pay and buy a pack of gum. It's also a friend's birthday, so you stop by the grocery store to pick up a gift certificate from their favorite restaurant. After breakfast with your friends, you have some meetings with colleagues and clients, some on the phone and some on Zoom calls. At 3:00, you pick up your kids from school and chat with a few other parents who are also waiting. At your kid's soccer practice, you chat with some more parents. Before you go home, you pick up some flowers for your significant other. You get home, have dinner with your spouse/partner and kids, make a quick phone call to a friend, and send text messages to others. After TV, you and your partner put the kids to bed and share a glass of wine before heading off.

You have opportunities to build Relationship Capital at every point in each interaction. Get to know that gas station clerk. Chat with the grocery store cashier, or maybe talk with someone in the store who's wearing your favorite team's baseball cap. Make sure to get to know your server meaningfully at breakfast with your friends. Ask one of your friends if they need help with something, especially if they're having a tough time. Ask some light personal questions with your associates and clients; nothing too personal, but something to show that you care about them as an individual.

You get the idea. The point is that whenever you are around another human being, that's an opportunity to make a deposit in your Relationship Capital account. Even if you never have (or need) to withdraw, you'll know that you're actively bringing bright moments to other people's days and lives. That little detail, that "Hello, how's it going? Need anything?" note, a smile, or a light conversation, can make the difference in your day and the other person's day.

Patching Holes

Making deposits in Relationship Capital is also a great way to patch holes in a friendship or business relationship. We all make mistakes, and when we do so where it affects another human being, the best thing we can do is show an effort to "fix" it.

A couple of years ago, I was invited to lunch with an influential podcaster. We knew each other casually but could have done better. So, I was looking forward to some time with him to get to know him and learn about what he does. Somehow, and I don't know how this happened, it didn't get on my calendar, and I just blew it off – I was a no-show. Since we had booked it a few weeks in advance, I somehow forgot about it, as we both carried on with our very busy lives.

Fortunately, this guy is a forgiving soul, and about a year later, he invited me to be on his podcast. So, of course, I agreed.

He paused on the phone and said, *"Just don't no-show me again."*

"What?"

I had no idea I had done this and felt terrible. I groveled a bit and told him, without a doubt, that I would be there. While talking, I put the date and time on my calendar. I apologized and sent a little gift basket. Six months later, I sent a quick text thanking him for the podcast opportunity again and apologizing for missing that initial lunch.

Was it too much? Maybe, but I wanted him to know I felt bad about screwing up. It was my way of showing him, not just telling him, that I was sorry.

When we take the time to patch holes in relationships, we're showing the other person that we care and own up to our mistakes. Sometimes this can send an even more powerful message than anything else, though I don't recommend being a "no-show" very often! If you screw up, own it and do something that demonstrates you're sorry. It's never too late to patch a hole, even years later.

Lance Moore

What does relationship capital mean to you, and how has it helped you?

Relationship capital is just as important or even more important than actual capital. Having that network and people you can lean on or tap into can pay dividends in numerous things.

Would you rather have $1,000,000 in cash or know 1,000 people well?

Is rather know 1,000 people well because tapping into that network can be much more fruitful than the $1,000,000 if properly worked.

Describe your relationship with Jeff Fenster.

Jeff and I are basketball buddies and have developed a more professional relationship through everbowl. I admire Jeff as an aspiring entrepreneur and look forward to building with him.

Build Your Relationship Capital

What opportunities did you miss yesterday?

_____

_____

_____

_____

_____

What opportunities can you take tomorrow?

_____

_____

_____

_____

_____

"Everyone you meet knows something you don't know but need to know. Learn from them."

C.G. Jung

Chapter 14

Cashing in Your Chips: Leveraging Relationship Capital

As we make deposits to our Relationship Capital accounts, in a very real way, we're "saving" just like we would for a financial account. As I first introduced at the beginning of this book, there are many parallels between money/spending and Relationship Capital. I want you to know that cashing in your Relationship Capital chips differs from spending willy-nilly and making withdrawals for silly "purchases."

At the same time, making withdrawals is a normal reality. Just as in life, you want to strategically make withdrawals, especially if you've made substantial investments. If you spend your money foolishly, you will have a negative balance. It's the same with relationships. If you make a stupid withdrawal by asking for a silly favor or making withdrawals by not respecting your friends, colleagues, and connections, you'll have a negative balance.

Often, there's a lot of fear around making a withdrawal. Like many people are anxious about money and spending money, many people are afraid to ask for favors. But I'm here to tell you that you must ask for favors and spend your Relationship Capital. There's a right and wrong way to do it, though.

Dumb Purchases/Clumsiness

Let's say you're walking down the street, and you take your keys out of your pocket. A $20 bill drops, but you don't notice and keep walking. Or let's say you're traveling and leave your wallet in the taxi, but when you get your wallet back, the $150 bucks in there is gone. When you're clumsy with your money, you will lose money. If you keep a close eye on where your wallet is and what money you have where you're unlikely to lose that cash.

In Relationship Capital, this shows up by being clumsy with your relationships. Maybe you start an Instagram page and get great responses to it. You're making connections, making daily posts that people are responding to, and you're also responding to others' posts and starting to make some meaningful relationships online. Then, you get bored with it after a couple of months and ignore the account for a few months. When you finally feel inspired again, you're following is ⅓ of what it was and not nearly as active and engaged.

In face-to-face relationships, the same thing can happen. You stop checking in with your friends, or you don't return phone calls and texts. You show up late to get-togethers and don't apologize for your behavior. You always talk about yourself and only listen on a very shallow level. When you're at work, you don't say "Hi" to anyone because you're "too busy." You're being clumsy with your friends. You're being clumsy with Relationship Capital and making withdrawals to your account. It's the equivalent of dropping that $20 bill or leaving your wallet behind.

You can also make withdrawals by spending money foolishly. For example, say you get a $50,000 settlement for an accident you were in a couple of years ago, so you buy a Lamborghini. Instead, you could use that money to make down payments on two investment properties. One's a smart purchase, and the other is dumb. Similarly, you can ask a friend to do a dumb favor ("Hey, call my wife, and help me play this trick on her,") or you could ask to connect with one of their contacts to advance your business. Again, one's a dumb use of Relationship Capital, and the other is very smart.

Use Your Network

We all live in a community, whether it's where our house is, our work community, our colleagues and clients, or our community of friends. We all need each other and depend on each other to one degree or another. As you make withdrawals from your Relationship Capital accounts, making deposits is important to replace any withdrawals. Don't be afraid to ask for help, support, or something that will strategically advance your efforts in work, business, or life.

If you don't ask your neighbor's father about help with your air conditioning system, don't you think he might feel a little put off by that? If you have a friend who's a travel agent, and you tell them about your upcoming trip that you spent hours online booking, how do you think they might feel? It's important to leverage our Relationship Capital with those we know. As long as we're not taking advantage of the person, they will probably really appreciate that they can help you somehow. When you ask them for advice or to make a connection for you, you're letting them know you appreciate what they do in life.

If I find that a "friend" has tapped into a different company for digital marketing, I might be a little upset. Mostly because I thought maybe we didn't have the relationship I thought we had. You might not even realize that it upsets me. Maybe you think you don't want to bother me, or you don't want to mix business with pleasure. If this is the case, think about how good you feel when someone asks for help, and you can truly help them out of a jam or help them advance in life.

Debt Can be Good

There is good debt and bad debt. Generally speaking, a car is a bad debt because it will never appreciate value. Generally, a home is a good debt because it will increase in value. Using your Relationship Capital can sometimes put you in debt with someone, and that's ok. Think of it as good debt. As you withdraw from them, think about how you can make it up to them. You might have a negative balance with them for a short time, but in the long term, you can build even more Relationship Capital with them as you continue to help each other out.

Just like with your money and finances, as long as you know how to get out of debt and refocus on savings once you make a big purchase, you'll be ok. With Relationship Capital, there is good debt and bad debt, just like with real money. So, take your Relationship Capital and reinvest with the person you are indebted to. Remember, it can just be sincere appreciation and a gift; humility and gratefulness go a long way for most people.

If you get into debt with someone and you have a negative Relationship Capital balance, just make sure you're reinvesting. Otherwise, you'll always be in debt, and you're just clumsy with that relationship. Whenever possible, create a relationship that feels like a win-win. You're either genuine in your relationships and interactions or not – there is no "mostly" or "some." You're either real or you're not. Be real.

Reverse Debt

This is a little tricky, but we've all probably been there on one end or another. This happens when someone is in debt in a relationship, but they blame the other person for that debt. An example I can think of off the top is if I give you a job. You bomb, and I must let you go, but I give you another chance. You blow that one, too. Finally, I give you a third chance, and I know this is the last time I'm sticking my neck out for you. You blow that one as well, so I have to fire you. You blame me for your failure, but the truth is that you've put yourself in debt with me over and over again.

Make sure to stop any bleeding. If you find yourself inadvertently in this position, start making some deposits with no expectations for anything, and carry on. Resentment for your own mistakes never works in the long or short term. It's easy to get into this mindset, so be honest if you've ever done this or are doing it now with anyone/anything in your life.

Bottom Line

Always, and I mean always, look at your relationship and new connections to make sure that you're being genuine. If you think, "What can they do for me?" you're always going to ultimately have a negative balance, even if you find initial success. People will only put up with that for so long.

Tony Whatley

What does relationship capital mean to you, and how has it helped you?

I grew up hearing the popular statement, "Success is all about who you know." I probably believed that until my mid-20s because I had nothing else to reference against it, and I didn't have enough experience to disprove it.

Nowadays, that statement is only half correct. Especially now that we've expanded our networks into digital space and social media. Our friend's network gets absolutely huge, numbering thousands of contacts. It isn't enough to just know others, as everyone seems to share that same potential. The missing half of that statement is that others must also know you, what you stand for, what value you create, and how a mutually beneficial relationship can be. It simply isn't enough to collect names; you must be willing to step out of the shadows and take actions that others will notice. You must create opportunities for them to know you.

Relationship capital isn't about transactions or thinking, "What's in it for me?" I see this as simply trying to do my best for others, always choosing to do the right thing. Investing your time and advice, cultivating relationships, and not expecting repayment. The more positive value I've put out into the world eventually comes back around somehow. We simply must make more positive deposits into this lifetime account than withdrawals.

Would you rather have $1,000,000 in cash or know 1,000 people well?

This may appear like an innocent, surface-level question, but it isn't. I've given this some thought rather than offering a knee-jerk response. While it would appear noble to turn away the financial aspect and claim some virtue by saying people mean more, I'll say that without full context - I'd take the cash.

"How dare you!" Some readers may think. But I'm known for being direct and honest. Who is to say that those 1,000 people are my type of people? They may be 1,000 toxic people or just insane people. Too many unknowns. At least the cash has no variables; it is what it is; A safe bet. I know the effort that went into earning my first million. It wasn't easy.

My perspective would change if I could select the 1,000 people I want to know well. Then I'd take those relationships.

Describe your relationship with Jeff Fenster.

I was introduced to Jeff in early 2019 and immediately admired his positive attitude and work ethic. I invited him to be a guest on my podcast, 365 Driven. He shared incredible insights and perspectives freely. Some guests require me to work hard to extract the "gold nuggets" they hold on to. Jeff was very forthcoming about his entrepreneurship adventures and failures, and successes. I knew after that interview that I'd like to keep in touch with him. In October 2020, I asked him to be a speaker at my first live speaking event to introduce him to my clients. He blew their minds with what he shared, and I'm certain he made friends with the entire audience that weekend. I look forward to Jeff's journey in life. So far, it's a great show.

Build Your Relationship Capital

Reflect on your current debts.

_____

_____

_____

_____

_____

How can you improve it?

_____

_____

_____

_____

_____

"A relationship is more of an assignment than a choice. We can walk away from the assignment, but we cannot walk away from the lessons it presents. So we stay with a relationship until a lesson is learned, or we simply learn it another way."

Marianne Williamson

Chapter 15

The Bug Light

I'm sure you've seen a bug light before – this special outdoor light with a bulb designed to attract bugs to it. Most of the time, that light draws the bugs away from another place or "zaps them." Of course, my analogy isn't EXACTLY like that, but the concept of the bug light can relate to Relationship Capital in a very simple way.

Basically, a bug light for our discussion is a light that's bigger and brighter than you. I don't mean as far as it comes to your intelligence, but sometimes that's the case, too, especially if you're a beginner. I mean that you can use your relationship with someone more well-known, established, popular, or famous than you are. For instance, I shared my story about attracting new clients to the digital marketing company because of my relationship with Neil Patel. I would tell potential clients how we could help and that I partner with Neil Patel. "If you don't know who he is, Google him and then tell me when you want to meet next week." I knew they would say "Yes," once they saw who I was working with, and sometimes I would tell them that.

Neil is my bug light.

The concept here is attraction marketing. You establish a relationship with someone who can be your bug light. The bug light can also be a company; you see this all the time on websites where it's prominently listed who else they've worked with. When you call a client, they say, "Oh, you've worked with Nike and Adidas?" Maybe not in so many words, but that status, credibility, and trust are established greatly because of your relationship with your bug-light person or company.

If you've ever gone to a concert, you've seen this in action. There's almost always an opening act that NEEDS the bug light of the bigger and brighter star to get in front of people. I know some concerts I've been to where I loved the opening act more than the headliner and became a big fan of theirs. In the business world, you can shine in someone else's big light by introducing their speech or making a speech before the keynote address. Maybe you know someone who has written several books, maybe even bestsellers, and you become a co-author with them. They already have the audience, and your name is forever next to theirs.

When you're first starting a new business, you'll need bug lights to help you get seen and noticed. Essentially, that person's light attracts other bugs to you so you can create your own ecosystem. You also magnify the strength of their own bug light for their own opportunities. In other words, if you're effective within their light, you're bringing even more bugs to their attention and audience – another win-win, which is what Relationship Capital is all about.

Now, I can't call up LeBron James (yet), and probably neither can you, but don't be discouraged. Start in your community with a local celebrity (maybe a newscaster) or with a community leader (the mayor, the head of the PTA, the president of a local philanthropic group like the Rotary Club, or a business organization like the chamber of commerce). Heck, start with your local high school star quarterback. We got great business from a high school across the street from our second Everbowl location. We sponsored a lunch for them, and they won that game. You know sports superstitions – they wanted to eat the same thing before their next game. They won. This went on for the next two games, eating at Everbowl, then winning. That introduced our product to a whole new audience. Now tons of kids from the high school and even their teachers eat at Everbowl because the football team was our bug light.

How bright is your bug light? Don't have one? Make a list of people you know who might be your bug light and look at them as a stepping stone to the next level. Constantly work your way up; maybe someday you'll be hanging in the same company as LeBron James or The Rock. Don't rule those possibilities out, but don't think you can start or even finish there. As long as you tap into someone at a higher level than you, you'll gain yards, notoriety, and status.

Scott Kaplan

What does relationship capital mean to you, and how has it helped you?

In 2007, a friend convinced me to get on a road bike for the first time in my life and ride with a group of 100 people from San Francisco to San Diego to raise $1 million for the Challenged Athletes Foundation.

On the first day of group training, I interviewed this friend for a series of videos we would eventually post about the cause, and what he said that day was deeper than I could have ever imagined.

To paraphrase, he said that morning, the relationships you will create on this journey will be lifelong friendships and business associations.

At the time, I thought, well, that sounds nice and very promotional for the event, but it's not likely true. In fact, I just took the statement as an embellishment. But, man, was I wrong.

That was thirteen years ago; the relationships created during that ride are truly for life. Not only did that ride change my life, but it also created relationships and opportunities.

Why? Because it wasn't 100 individuals riding their bikes 750 miles over 7 days for pleasure. Rather, it was 100 people collectively suffering for a cause. This was bigger than a bike ride; it was about empowering physically challenged people who were simultaneously inspiring us with their willingness to do the same work with fewer physical resources. These people, essentially strangers then, have become lifelong friends, teammates, business partners, and motivators in my life and business.

When my friend said relationships for life, he could not have been more right.

When people understand what you are made of, what you are willing to do, and how far you are willing to go, not just for yourself but for others, you create a level of trust.

Ultimately, these relationships have become my closest friends, who motivated me to reach outside my comfort zone and become a startup entrepreneur, and they became supporters and investors.

That is relationship capital for me.

Would you rather have $1,000,000 in cash or know 1,000 people well?

To know 1000 people well is a very hard thing to do. So first, think about the phrase; you reflect the five people you are closest to. Then try to expand your top 5 to your top 10, then expand to your top 20; it starts to get really hard.

Look at your Facebook page; how many friends do you have, and how many do you know well?

Here's my point, 1000 relationships with people you know well would be worth more than $1 million.

Think if you were starting a business. If you had $1 million, it would be a good start, but if you had 1000 people you knew well, you would be able to generate so much more than $1 million, be it through fundraising or those same people supporting your business with their patronage.

If given a choice, I would take the relationships because they are more personally fulfilling and worth way more money!

My philosophy is Net Worth equals network!

Describe your relationship with Jeff Fenster.

I have huge admiration and love for Jeff Fenster.

I love that Jeff shares a relentless attitude; he has the energy that screams nothing can stop him!

Not only is he a successful entrepreneur, but he is also a selfless giver of what he knows or what he is learning along the way.

Jeff could be exclusively ultra-focused on his business, but he is willing to inspire, not just within his company, but for the outside world of people looking for examples of 'if he can do it, so can I!'

Another personality trait I admire about Jeff is his willingness to take a risk. He was very successful at a young age. Rather than get comfortable and pigeonholed into being one thing, Jeff essentially decided to do something on a whim, but his energy turned that whim into a monster business and brand.

He could have taken his money and run when his next venture became a huge hit. That's not Jeff. What did he do? He took his success and thought, how can I help other up-and-coming entrepreneurs start their own businesses and add value to others in many ways.

Truly an amazing businessman, father, husband, son, friend, and motivator to so many people.

Build Your Relationship Capital

Who is your bug light?

_____

_____

_____

_____

_____

Who are some bug lights that you want to become more acquainted with?

_____

_____

_____

_____

_____

"Friendship is not a noun. Friendship is a verb, a process, an art."

Kyler Shumway

Chapter 16

Become an Expert

By leveraging the expertise of others, either via the light bug concept or through your Relationship Capital, you can become your own expert and someone else's bug light. For instance, with this book, with my course, speaking on podcasts, and at events, I'm putting myself as an expert or authority on Relationship Capital. It happens when you put information and content into a subject matter related to your passion and learning experiences. Then, as more and more people hear me talk or read my blogs, they see me as an expert in the field where I work. It's an organic process to become an expert, even though you're making deliberate strides to get from point A to point B.

It's like climbing a mountain; think of the peak as the ultimate reputation as the authority on the topic. You can't buy your way up there – you can't hire a helicopter to drop you off at the top – otherwise, you'd be laughed off the summit. The only way to get to the top, and be seen as an expert, is to climb your way up, one step at a time. You can lighten your backpack through Relationship Capital, so it's easier to get there. You don't see many solo treks to the top of Mt. Everest because it requires team effort and support. The same applies to reaching that professional summit – I think it can only happen through Relationship Capital. You leverage those relationships and that Relationship Capital to get to the peak.

This expands your Relationship Capital even further because it expands your reach and your exposure even more. From there, Relationship Capital is amassed even more, and the more you interact as the expert, the higher you can climb. There may be only room for one Tony Robbins or one Michael Jordan, but we all can name several experts in their field who have amassed a high degree of expertise and talent. They all got there on the backs of others. When you have Relationship Capital and lots of friends, their backs aren't burdened any more than a grown man's back is burdened as he carries his little girl's backpack – it's a piece of cake, and he's proud and happy to help.

As you continue to climb, you will rub shoulders with the people you aspire to be like. You'll continue to develop relationships with brighter and brighter bug lights and more and more influential individuals. It all starts with those initial steps and honoring the concept of Relationship Capital. As you become more "valuable," it opens up more opportunities for you and chances to rise/climb even further. Slowly but surely, you become your own bug light – this is the ultimate goal. You start leveraging others to build your own ecosystem, so now you're the expert in your field. You don't need anyone else's bug light because others are leveraging yours. Instead of always working on getting to meet someone at a higher level, you're a gatekeeper of sorts for others to meet some of your connections and to meet you.

When tapping into this, it's almost like residual or passive income to Relationship Capital that you've built up over time. You're receiving as much as you're giving when you're at this level, and it feels great. For example, Warren Moon built great notoriety as a quarterback via the Minnesota Vikings, Seattle Seahawks, and Houston Oiler's organizations. His name recognition and brand value skyrocketed by being associated with these organizations. He leveraged their bug lights to become his own bug light. Likewise, David Meltzer, my mentor, leveraged the bug light of Warren Moon to become his own bug light. Likewise, I tapped into David Meltzer's bug light to become my expert and authority in Relationship Capital. As I've mentioned, this is the game's name – we're all in this together.

It's the hierarchy of Relationship Capital. It's also never-ending and, in many ways, is just another version of the game of life. You can become an expert on several levels and in several ways, depending on your expertise. Maybe you can be an expert in natural health and nutrition. You can also be an expert on Relationship Capital and leveraging relationships to market your educational content. As you continue to become an expert, you find yourself next to even brighter bug lights. For example, Everbowl and I showed up on the marketing materials right next to Chipotle and Starbucks for an upcoming conference on fast-casual restaurants. So, I'll leverage that association as I continue growing our profile. I'm rubbing shoulders with some of the biggest names in the industry just four years after starting Everbowl and speaking on the same stage as them. This is all 100% a result of leveraging Relationship Capital.

You don't have to be amazing at anything to do this. You can be good, maybe even mediocre. I don't have a rocket-scientist brain. Honestly, I don't know much about restaurants, but I know what I like to eat, what I want to see in a restaurant, and how to put that together. Maybe that makes me an expert, but it's not like I'm the end-all of restaurant management and growth. I'm just a guy who has leveraged Relationship Capital with humility, honesty, and sincerity to advance my knowledge in the field. The skill of making friends can open doors to becoming an expert alongside the tops in the field.

People seek experts. You can then attract the people you want by being an expert. You learn your craft deeply when you teach it, so putting yourself out there as the expert and teaching your expertise, will sharpen your skills even more. When you break into an industry, figure out how to become an expert and eventually rub shoulders with the best of the best.

At the same time, it's important to know when to pivot. I was an amateur boxer and worked hard at the craft, but it became clear that I needed to do something else. I recognized that I probably wasn't going to become a pro that made millions of dollars. Yes, there's room at the top for lots of people, but you have to be honest when it's time to move on or pivot to something that you'll be able to do better. When it came to boxing, I didn't love it enough to sacrifice what it took to become a top player. Two broken noses later, I realized I was doing it more for my grandfather than myself.

To become a true expert, you have to be extremely passionate about it so that you're willing to do the work and enjoy it. When you're passionate, it's much easier to develop expertise. For example, before I go to sleep, I plan my business. I don't sing in the shower; I plan. I'm passionate about business, Relationship Capital, and entrepreneurship, so it's "easier" for me to develop expertise on the topic.

Success is almost a foregone conclusion when you're an expert in your field. However, people will find you, and your Relationship Capital will speed all of this up.

Josh York

What does relationship capital mean to you, and how has it helped you?

Relationship capital is the most important part of achieving success. You must plant a seed and water it every day for that plant to grow and be strong. By building relationships, you can move the needle forward in any business. This has helped me in my life in so many different ways I could take hours writing it! I will give you one example. I had the pleasure of having Jeff on my podcast, and from that single interaction and establishing this relationship, he has now invited me to contribute to his book!

If you build relationship capital, you will have many opportunities!

Would you rather have $1,000,000 in cash or know 1,000 people well?

Easy answer; I would rather know 1,000 people very well. Those 1,000 people can help open doors for you to make that million dollars into a whole lot more. Not to mention the wonderful friendships one can build along the way. PRICELESS!

Describe your relationship with Jeff Fenster.

Jeff and I love taking long walks in the park and eating Everbowl. He will discuss all the ingredients in each bowl and explain the reasoning behind why it tastes so darn good! (this is a joke, people, just for a good smile)

(I like the joke…but for sensitivity reasons, you may want to take out the "long walks in the park" portion and keep the food discussion portion and home in on that comedy. But, on the other hand, it could alienate some audiences. Unsure who is actually reading these answers.)

Jeff was a guest on my podcast FUEL YOUR DRIVE. Since that episode aired, we have built a solid relationship, and I am very happy and honored to call him my friend.

Build Your Relationship Capital

What are your initial steps?

_____

_____

_____

_____

_____

How can you become an expert?

_____

_____

_____

_____

_____

"Friendships can happen any 'where' and any 'when' – you never know how the next one will come about!"

Lucy Lane

Final Thoughts

Friendship is the goal!

By now, I've harped on this enough, and I think you get my point. So what I want to do here is to challenge you a little. First, take stock of who your friends are. Who do you know and like in your business and personal life? How old are they? What do they look like? Do they look like you? Most of the time, our network could almost be a mirror. We tend to hang around with people who look like us, talk like us, and dress like us. This is boring and limiting. I challenge you to make sure that you are expanding your network to include people who are older than you, younger than you, who speak a different language, or who live in a different part of town than you. Look for people you can build sincere relationships with, but they may dress differently than you or mix in the same circles.

I've touched on this early, but today's divisive world serves no one. Instead, we must connect and get to know people and respect people with different viewpoints, backgrounds, goals, dreams, and passions.

We will take great care of each other as we develop our friendships and expand our reach and network. We can all get to know people and be friends with individuals different from us. From there, we'll expand who we are as individuals.

Yes, this book is about leveraging Relationship Capital to build your business, get that meeting, and make that connection. The bigger idea is to use the ideas in this book to leverage the power of relationships in life. The business is a side gig, almost. Business comes last in conversation. I want to talk less about business than my friends, even as passionate as I am about business and entrepreneurship. I want to talk about things that strengthen my friendships. Business is easy, but great friendships take more work to come by.

Focus on friendship first. The rest will follow.

On a final note, always remember the power of four minutes. You can change your life in four minutes. A simple four-minute conversation with a grocery store clerk can change your life. A four-minute meeting with a new person can introduce you to your husband or wife. Four minutes of listening and learning can open your eyes and heart to new opportunities. The four-minute window of time can open up your whole life. There are no limits, and four minutes can get you from here to there. So use every four-minute gift that you can; learn to recognize when something special that seems ordinary is happening. Engage in conversation with that person at the airport. Take that phone call from a friend of a friend. You never know what the next four minutes might bring.

Andre Rush (Chef Rush)

What does relationship capital mean to you and how has it helped you in your life?

Relationship capital is the embodiment of not only customer to vender, but a bond that is developed with trust, respect and hard work from both sides.

Would you rather have $1,000,000 in cash or know 1,000 people very well?

I knew 1,000 people very well, they didn't make me a million dollars. And that million dollars can help me support 10,000 people.

Describe your relationship with Jeff Fenster.

Our relationship is built off of mutual respect first for who the individual is. Friendship is an understatement as we learn abs grow frim each other no matter how small or big. I have always respect his drive and passion towards business as well as the fellow entrepreneur.

Andy Nguyen

What does relationship capital mean to you and how has it helped you in your life?

Relationship capital to me means it's important to have an emotional connection with others. And to me it's been the far most valuable thing to me in business.

Would you rather have $1,000,000 in cash or know 1,000 people very well?

I would rather know 1,000 great people very well. It's priceless.

Describe your relationship with Jeff Fenster.

Jeff is someone I highly admire. He's a very knowledgeable person, and if he doesn't know the answer; he'll figure it out sooner than you think.

Bo Hawkins

What does relationship capital mean to you and how has it helped you in your life?

I learned long ago that relationships were the most important skill in life. I was basically homeless and not surrounded by the best influence. When I decided to hack my circle of friends to be better, I noticed my life began to change drastically.

That eye rolling meme of "You're the average of your 4 friends" is more true than we ever realise. I've dedicated my life to learning how to improve relationships and "raise my capital". Like any great skill, there are key points to mastering connecting and networking that we can all learn.

I wouldn't be where I am today without the exceptional relationships I have, which allows me to live a dream life that's constantly growing.

Would you rather have $1,000,000 in cash or know 1,000 people very well?

I would take it even further, I'd rather know 10 people very well instead of $1,000,000, because with 10 people I know very well, that million dollar ceiling disappears. Also, money's just money. You can have a much better life knowing the right people. Those living a great life, doing what they love… the money tends to follow.

Describe your relationship with Jeff Fenster.

I felt I knew Jeff before we ever even spoke. So many people in mutual circles had told me about Jeff and what a great, welcoming guy he was. This is really important to realise, because how you treat others echoes into social circles and can create opportunities that you never even knew. I'm very blessed to know Jeff and completely align with his principles on relationships.

Brian Augustine

What does relationship capital mean to you and how has it helped you in your life?

To me relationship capital ties directly into the Golden Rule. Treating others the way you wish to be treated. In business and in business relationships, people want to work with those they know, like and trust. Currently, there is a lot of conversation out there about adding value to the relationship. Important as it may be, if your relationship isn't built off of trust, the value will only go so far and be worth so much. Some people are gifted in building trust quickly, it comes naturally to them. They are the collaborators and the connectors. I believe these are the people who utilize relationship capital to their fullest extent. To its highest and best place in their life. Who they know will be how they grow, and they accomplish leveraging resources in their network without applying pressure. They are in flow with their sphere.

Would you rather have $1,000,000 in cash or know 1,000 people very well?

I would rather have $1,000,000 in cash and put the funds to use and perhaps get to know 1000 people very well. If you come into the game with light pockets, you are forcing or trying to build relationships. The $1m will open doors, get you connected, and in theory, bring about opportunities otherwise unavailable.

Describe your relationship with Jeff Fenster.

My relationship with Jeff is relatively new, but highly valued. I would consider Jeff one of those high caliber types and I am grateful to know him. I am excited to get to know him better and watch how he will further impact the world.

Jeff and I have been working together since March of 2017. We both share similar values, intense mindset and have a strong belief in what we are doing, Everbowl or not.

The road to get to where everbowl has gone has few directional signs, no pavement and definitely no speed limit! Through it all, we were able to keep standards high, live by our Core Values and understand the need to push each other at certain key moments. This was not accomplished without butting heads and without a few pissed off moments. Those situations should happen and will continue to happen when you are going hard in this type of environment. I think over the last 12 months and being in our space for several years, has opened his eyes to what it takes to keep 25 locations going.

At no point have we ever settled, gotten too high on our horse nor been too disappointed when something didn't work out. We are able to talk about every aspect of the business weekly if not daily, specifically how to maintain a world class culture, in an ongoing effort to provide a top notch experience for our customers and the local kids we employ. Jeff and I are teammates who trust each other along with 250 others moving the ball downfield, expecting effort and enthusiasm everyday in all we do. Being relentless in a pursuit of going from good to great.

Carlos Reyes

What does relationship capital mean to you and how has it helped you in your life?

Relationship capital has been a game changer in our real estate investing business. It's allowed us flexibility and freedom. Since securing private capital we've been to acquire more properties and expand into other markets across the country.

Would you rather have $1,000,000 in cash or know 1,000 people very well?

I would rather know 1,000 people very well. By knowing 1,000 people very well there is a high probability that you can raise far more than 1,000,000 dollars. Your network is your net worth.

Describe your relationship with Jeff Fenster.

Jeff is a reputable individual and business man. Our principles and core values align and I'm looking forward to seeing what the future holds for us on a personal level and on a business level.

Casey Adams

What does relationship capital mean to you and how has it helped you in your life?

Relationship capital to me means the connection and access to valuable people in your life. When I say "valuable," I'm referring to the value that each individual can bring to you for a specific goal. When I was 15 years old I was almost paralyzed playing football, and this injury changed the direction of my life forever. I began studying successful entrepreneurs and ultimately decided to go all in on my goals. Early on I heard the quote, "your network is your net worth," and it stuck with me. Since 16 years old I've been focused on building a world class network in my life. Originally I started connecting with successful people on social media and that's what led me to starting my podcast, Rise of The Young. Over the past three years I've interviewed over 300+ high level entrepreneurs and CEO's including, Larry King, Maye Musk, Rick Ross, Tilman Fertitta, Robert Greene, and many more. Having a podcast has increased my relationship capital more than anything else in my life. Relationships to me are everything, each person in my life has a unique skillset and we always try to help each other. Without the quality relationships in my life I'm not sure where I'd be along my journey.

Would you rather have $1,000,000 in cash or know 1,000 people very well?

As a twenty year old entrepreneur I've always placed so much value on my network. Like I said before, my podcast has created so many incredible relationships in my life and to me they are worth way more than $1,000,000 in cash long term. When it comes to knowing 1,000 people very well, to me it really comes down to the quality of people. Having incredible people in my life can help me raise money for a new startup, create deal flow, introduce me to other quality people, and those connections are priceless. Every great business has great people, and knowing 1,000 great people to me is worth much more than $1,000,000.

Describe your relationship with Jeff Fenster.

My relationship with Jeff Fenster has been incredible. I originally met him at an event we were both speaking at in Los Angeles. Right away we connected and he happens to be one of the most genuine people I know. The way he thinks about business is incredible and I learned so much from him when I had him on my podcast. Ever since we met I've been following his journey with Everbowl, and his execution is next level. He's been able to put together an amazing team, and I have so much respect for his ability to build a great culture in his organization. Every time I walk into Everbowl I have a great experience and the employees make you feel so welcomed. Jeff is a mentor to me and somebody that I look forward to building with long term.

Dan Fulkerson

What does relationship capital mean to you and how has it helped you in your life?

Relationship capital is the power of your network and your ability to be able to call on your network to help you execute your goals. For myself, I'm a personal injury attorney but I have always marketed myself as the guy you call no matter what you need because I'll help find the right person for you. By doing so, it's added a lot of value to myself and my reputation, but also enabled me to expand my network by referring other business owners quality leads and referrals. The result has been a vast and strong network that contributes value to my businesses and my personal life on a daily basis.

Would you rather have $1,000,000 in cash or know 1,000 people very well?

Depends on who the 1,000 people are. I'd pick knowing 10 of the right people well, over a million cash.

Describe your relationship with Jeff Fenster.

True story: I met Jeff when he opened his first Everbowl store and had started to look for investors for expansion. Anyone who meets with Jeff is impressed but when he told me how quickly he planned to roll out stores, and the number of stores he wanted to roll out Year 1 of expansion, I thought it was over ambitious and I passed on the investment. Well, I was wrong. Jeff did everything he said he was going to do. At some point, I pulled him aside and let him know I was wrong and regretted passing on the opportunity. For me it's a life lesson and was fortunate enough to get a good friend out of it.

Eric Siu

What does relationship capital mean to you and how has it helped you in your life?

Relationship capital to me is having meaningful relationships with likeminded people. It has helped me approach relationships with a long term mindset instead of 'networking' with people. Without it, there's no way I would have been able to have the success that I've had so far.

Would you rather have $1,000,000 in cash or know 1,000 people very well?

1,000 people very well, easy. Worth way more than the $1M in cash in my opinion.

Describe your relationship with Jeff Fenster.

Jeff is a relationship machine. He doesn't just try to rack up as many 'relationships' as possible, he actually shows that he cares about you. He knows keep the quality of his network high and is a master of relationship capital.

Erich Broesel

What does relationship capital mean to you and how has it helped you in your life?

For me Relationship Capital means never losing a chance to make a friend. It means building bridges wherever you go. For me friendships are just like bridges. They connect special things, covering gaps of companionship, emotional support, camaraderie and loneliness. We can also lean on a good friendship to bridge the gaps of opportunity.

I grew up competing in what people called a dead-end sport. Perhaps all sports are for most are "dead-end." But no matter the game, sports give us valuable life assets. Along with the grit, self-esteem and self-reliance that comes from competing with friends, comes the gift of the relationships that develop in the process. My "dead-end" sport turned out to be my most valuable business bridge. Literally all except for one, of my most impactful business relationships can be traced back to friendships I made as a kid racing, in my "dead-end" sport.

Interestingly, the one out-standing relationship that did not come from my childhood sport, did come from my kids' participation in sport. That relationship is with Jeff Fenster. Our kids play soccer together!

Would you rather have $1,000,000 in cash or know 1,000 people very well?

For their thousand possibilities, I'd take the friends.

Three reasons:

1. While I strive to be multidimensional, I need my expert friends! I keep a Go-To list. I need a friend who knows operations. A friend who knows how to manage people. I need a friend for product development. One for photography, one for media production. For IT, PR, HR... I definitely need a CFO friend. The list goes on and on. And yes, I would want my financial advisor friend to help manage the 1M anyway!!

2. The right friend can inspire new possibilities to live into. Leveraging relationships solves entrepreneurial problems you encounter, but it also can solve entrepreneurial problems you create. I actually find myself dreaming up new ideas just because of the new friend I made!

3. Let's face it, if you're pursuing success for the right reasons, one of them should be - to have a lot of friends, another - to have (and give) a lot of love. Love and friendship go hand-in-hand and although we sometimes don't realize it, nothing feels as good as the exchange of help.

Describe your relationship with Jeff Fenster.

Haha, along with a lot of emails littered with happy-face emojis, my relationship with Jeff has been a blueprint-manifestation of everything you hear him talk about. At work, he's a walking library of idioms. He has this thing he says about wanting to surround himself with a team where he's always the dumbest guy in the room. It's funny, he does do that! Sometimes I have to tell him, "nooo - you're just playing dumb! I actually value your opinion and I need it right now!" It's been really fun working with him; he trusts my judgement so we never get stuck in revision mode. Because of that we can go incredibly fast together. He just knows when to micromanage and with the team we have, he almost never has to.

And if you're wondering, we are "actual friends" away from the office as well! We hang out almost weekly and shoptalk is never off-the-table! We really do enjoy our work together so when we hang it finds its way into the mix without wrecking the vibe. I think part of Jeff's thing about being able to integrate friends and business, is being able to integrate "just a little" shoptalk into your down-time. Now if we could get our wives to enjoy that as much as we do, we'd be in super good shape!

JJ

What does relationship capital mean to you and how has it helped you in your life?

Every brand I've ever built or ever helped has been built off of relationship capital because of my Authenticity. People know for me to get behind something I have to have passion.

Would you rather have $1,000,000 in cash or know 1,000 people very well?

1,000 people very well because I'm going to make more then a million.

Describe your relationship with Jeff Fenster.

We met thru a meeting and that hustlers spirit connected. You know when somebody has the same work ethic as you it's the sparkle in their eye he has that 😎.

Stephen Scoggins

What does relationship capital mean to you and how has it helped you in your life?

After 22 years of bootstrapping and building businesses from the trenches of the everyday fight to the stability of building profitable and unified organizations. I have discovered that every venture large or small will succeed or fail based on its ability to build, develop, and scale relational capital. When I think back to all of the high-value success I can always trace it back to one handshake, a meal over a barbeque, or any other time where I can come along with someone in the of service. And it never fails that those who know you care about their outcome also share in the hopes and dreams of the outcomes I desire to reach. Conversely, many of the ultimate business challenges that I have faced over the twenty-plus years come down to partnering with those with low standards and integrity.

This means not only is relational capital important to scale, but it's also always in need of consistent discernment. In short, relationships will make or break any goal, ambition, or endeavor. Which is why Jeff's work is so vitally important.

Would you rather have $1,000,000 in cash or know 1,000 people very well?

If you would have asked me in my early days as an entrepreneur I likely would have sought the $1,000,000.00 dollar seed investment based on needs because I was focused on the immediate. I am so thankful that I never got the seed money I was always craving and I was forced to build all of my businesses from cash. And instead, I got something far more valuable, "Mentors". Mentors that open doors of opportunity, built me up, challenged me to rise, and held me accountable. They taught me how to build more than a business. They taught me to build myself so that I could build others. When other people sense that you are sincere about helping their advancement, just as my mentors did for me, there is just something special about how it inspires a greater sense of personal value. Nothing gets built unless a relationship does first and experience has taught me that 1,000 people who come alongside you is dump truck levels of future revenue. I also believe the trick is not getting lost in the short cuts during the process. A short cut may allow you to win for a moment but will also cost you a lifetime of relational capital for the future.

Describe your relationship with Jeff Fenster.

I believe that true Entrepreneurs recognize true entrepreneurs and as a result can since but sacrifice and experience. Jeff has no shortage of both. I would describe my relationship with Jeff as an ever-growing example of how entrepreneurs can join together and change the world in a positive way. Jeff's insights on relational capital are needed more than ever in order to change the tied of the "use-ary" that can happen all too often in and around the business. We can all learn a lot from his thought leadership in this area for sure and scale it over time as we put his teachings into practice. Jeff, is a one of kind walking Billboard of how entrepreneurship should be done day in and day out. And I am looking forward to a continually growing relationship with Jeff as a student as well as a fellow entrepreneur.

FREE GIVEAWAY

Get your copy of Jeff's Network to Millions Playbook

Just scan above to instantly get access!!